TAKING BACK
AMERICA

DENNA LORRAINE

TAKING BACK AMERICA: CAMPAIGN SECRETS I LEARNED BATTLING NANCY PELOSI AND THE SWAMP, HOW TO BE A FEARLESS FIREBRAND FOR AMERICA'S FUTURE

DeAnnaLorraine.com

In Association with:
Elite Online Publishing
63 East 11400 South Suite #230
Sandy, UT 84070
EliteOnlinePublishing.com

Editor: Eileen Ansel Conery

Printed in the United States of America

ISBN: 978-1513660523

TABLE OF CONTENTS

★ ★ ★

★ ★ ★

Make sure that you're a part of my growing community of fearless patriots as we fight together in the war of our lives to take back America. Join my Inner Circle email list and Telegram group - *this is our "safe space" to freely communicate about all of these issues, organize, mobile rallies and other important actions that we need to take to fight back & take back America:*
DeannaLorraine.com/inner-circle.

Also be sure you subscribe to my Podcast, **Taking Back America!** *I broadcast every* Tuesday, Wednesday & Thursday *from* **YouTube**, **Periscope, iTunes,** *and other channels and I keep you updated on the latest breaking news as well as my upcoming events.*

YouTube.com/c/DeAnnaLorraine

Twitter.com/DeAnna4Congress

DEDICATION

This book is dedicated to my dear friend, Marc Angelucci. Marc was a fierce warrior for truth and justice. He was a high-profile Men's and Father's Rights attorney, and one of the founders of the National Coalition For Men. I met him during my activism work in the Men's Rights community and I immediately saw his kindness, huge heart, and dedication to justice. He was tragically killed while this book went to print, on July 11th, 2020. He was fighting for America, fighting to restore justice to men, fathers, and families, and sharing many truths that unfortunately made him a threat to the Swamp. The Swamp is very real, and the casualties caused by them are the many reasons why we must fight them and we must fight to take back our country.

Marc, you will be missed. Rest in peace.

PREFACE

"Older men declare war. But it is youth that must fight and die. And it is youth who must inherit the tribulation, the sorrow, and the triumphs that are the aftermath of war."
— **Herbert Hoover**

Running for Congress, being an outspoken Conservative activist and sharing my experiences and insights through my writing and journalistic work has been the path I felt called to take in order to make a positive impact in the future of America. This book will help you if you have any interest in running for public office, but also can help bolster your leadership and activism in all capacities. Perhaps you feel called to start an organization or non-profit that promotes a cause about which you're passionate. Or maybe you want to teach, speak, or just be a bolder and more prominent influencer in your area of expertise or ministry. Whether you wish to make a difference in a more subtle way or become a totally visible political firebrand, my intention for this book is to help you make a major impact and become a wildly successful warrior that is badly needed in our country right now. We need an army of fearless warriors with fire and energy, who are going to defend our president and fight to take our country back! The future of America depends on *you*.

Before you begin the book, I first want to define these terms as they will be relevant throughout:

Fearless: Bold, brave, courageous, valiant. Being "fearless" doesn't necessarily mean you don't ever *feel* fear, but as you *recognize* fear, you have the courage and strength to *face* the fear.

There is *"Nothing to fear but Fear Itself"* — **Franklin D. Roosevelt**

Firebrand: a person who is passionate about a particular cause, typically inciting change and taking radical revolutionary action.

"The most powerful weapon on earth is the human soul on fire." — **Ferdinand Foch**

I want to be clear that I am not a "seasoned campaign manager" nor "expert." I simply am sharing my personal journey, experience, lessons, and strategies that worked for me, that I believe will benefit you. I also made mistakes and learned some valuable lessons along the way, which I think are important to share. Certain things I discuss that worked for me may not be effective for you. There is not necessarily a one-size-fits-all strategy for running a winning campaign, but I do hope my experiences help you. — **DeAnna Lorraine**

INTRODUCTION

"In love we find out who we want to be;
in war we find out who we are."
— **Kristin Hannah, *The Nightingale***

I just went through a war. I am bloody, bruised, and beaten. I'm clutching my covers, shivering in a onesie, because I'm also fighting off what appears to be pneumonia from all those final nights spent knocking on doors in the freezing cold, or maybe even coronavirus from shaking too many hands and kissing too many babies on the campaign trail.

Alas, I am alive. I survived this war. In fact, I'm more alive than ever and ready to talk about it.

Let's flashback to 2019 for a minute. My two big goals for the year: find my future husband AND make a positive impact in my country. "Fighting The Swamp" wasn't quite on my list. Yet.

I was enjoying being a commentator on the news, hosting my podcast, and speaking at events. In 2018 I published my first book, *Making Love Great Again*.[1] No, it's not a cheesy book about sex or "making love!" It's actually just the opposite: a highly political book that addresses how Marxist, liberal ideologies and practices have destroyed not only our country as a whole, but our culture, our relationships, and the family unit. I share my story of how I came to be such a fierce advocate for Conservative values and an outspoken critic of liberalism and feminism. I had seen how the left had been systematically corrupting our values and removing God from our culture. I had been disgusted with the Left weakening boys and men as a means to destabilize nations, so we would be easier to control and more dependent on the government. Growing up with four brothers and working closely with males in my coaching practice, I have become a huge advocate for males and fathers and have witnessed the unique challenges they've been facing in recent decades due to the rise in misandry and male-bashing feminism. What most women and feminists didn't seem to understand is that by demonizing and weakening boys and men, women are actually hurt the most in the long-run.

I am also a child of divorced parents and although I'm very close with my amazing family, I had a tough childhood at times due to the divorce and moving around a lot. It made me realize later on just how important having a strong family is, both in our personal lives, and in the country as a whole. I had been considering starting a nonprofit organization to promote strengthening our culture and the family unit and raise awareness about these issues. As I always say, strong families and strong relationships create a strong country.

Everything changed one night when I put up a simple tweet. It was during the period when Nancy started really pushing for President Trump's impeachment and constantly knocking down his attempts to clean up our corrupt immigration system. I was so frustrated with Nancy and her constant blockading of our president's agenda. It was becoming abundantly clear that she prioritized illegal immigrants and asinine issues over American citizens and the *real* issues that really matter to us. At the time, I was in Washington DC for the big CPAC conference, and I was one of many patriots who stormed into Nancy's office with signs demanding that she be labeled a "Traitor to America." My friend Marjorie Greene actually started this petition, which included thousands of signatures when we presented it to Nancy's office assistant.

That night I put up a tweet that said, *"I'm considering running for Congress against Nancy Pelosi in California, District-12."* I put it up there not really taking it too seriously at the time. But to my surprise, the tweet instantly was picked up and retweeted thousands of times, garnering tons of enthusiasm and support. It drew a lot of media attention, which resulted in many interviews over the course of several weeks.

'Me, run for Congress? No. That's crazy!' I thought. I entertained the idea and of course I had considered it, otherwise I wouldn't have put up the tweet, but it just seemed like so much work and such a "big" undertaking that required so much, I didn't think I was really capable of it. I always thought of someone "running for Congress" as an elite, Ivy League graduate type with deeply entrenched political parents who had been groomed for political office their whole life.

The more I thought about it, though, the more it nagged at me. Why *can't* I though? Why *don't* I? I've always been a bit of a rebel throughout my life. I've never followed the herd and I've always questioned things and thought outside the box. My rebellious streak has been both a blessing and a curse — it's hindered me at times, but also served me well — more positively lately as people are waking up and looking for leaders who speak the truth, regardless of the potential social backlash.

I just sat on the idea for a while. I waited... and waited. I thought, surely someone else was going to announce that they'd run against Nancy for Congress, right? Surely some big name public figure or uber qualified candidate would announce any day now that they're running against her, I thought, but... no one did.

I thought about the kind of change I really could make if I actually was working in Congress, rather than just talking about issues on the sidelines. I thought about my platform, which would enable me to talk more in depth about the issues I already had been championing, but with much greater reach and impact.

I thought about the timing, and how in all honesty if I wanted to have a family of my own in the next few years, the period I had now in front of me, with me being unattached with lots of free time may not be the same in the next election cycle. I thought about how crucial the next election of 2020 would be, and how we simply could not afford to elect any more RINOs, Alexandria Ocasio-Cortez (AOC)-style Socialists, and slimy traitors into office that would continue to sabotage President Trump's agenda.

I thought about how we absolutely needed true patriots in office who would be bold, honest, loyal, and who would fearlessly fight for Americans and for the American principles that we so desperately needed to preserve before it was too late. It did seem like the next logical step.

I started getting approached by more and more people. Random people on social media would send me messages telling me, "Please, run against Nancy! Run against that old witch, you would be such a great asset in Congress!" Other colleagues and friends in my political social circles also kept reaching out and encouraging me to run, promising to help and support me if I decided to go for it.

However, it just seemed so... BIG. So DAUNTING. One friend connected me to a campaign consultant and encouraged me to call him. After we spoke, he was very excited about the prospect of me running and told me how confident he was that my campaign would be a success if he worked with me.

I was still pretty indecisive and nervous, to be honest, but nevertheless, we went ahead and filed my initial campaign forms, quietly, just so I could get that step out of the way in case I decided to run.

It wasn't until one day in August when I finally confirmed my decision to run. I was invited to speak at an established and popular men's conference, the International Conference on Men's Issues. What most women and feminists didn't seem to understand is that when feminists demonize and weaken boys and men, it affects women significantly, too. In the long-run, a culture of weakened men actually hurt women more.

Throughout the weekend conference, I had many conversations with the attendees. Some of their experiences brought me to tears. When it came time for my big speech, I opened by reading an op-ed I wrote entitled, *"Dear Father,"* where I talked about the negative impact of my parents' divorce on me as well as why fathers and men are so important and needed in our world, unlike what the left has us believe through their constant misandric messaging.

At the end of my speech, I was so moved and inspired by the audience's positive reaction that it compelled me to announce it then and there. My decision was made. I said, "Thank you so much for listening... AND... I have actually decided to run for Congress, so I can truly help bring about change in these areas and push these issues into the forefront of importance again in our country." The watery eyes in the room turned into hopeful eyes. Then I added, "And... I'm going to be running against Nancy Pelosi in California's twel..." before I could even finish the sentence, I got a massive uproar of applause and the entire room erupted in a standing ovation, clapping and cheering. Everyone was so excited. I realized then that I was going to do this and I was committed to the cause, because it wasn't about *me*. It was no longer about little old *me* and my fears and worries that I had been stalling over. It was about something much bigger than just *me*.

I was on a much bigger mission. This was about highlighting important issues in America that had long been swept under the rug. This was about finally having an honest national discussion about the state of the American family, about the state of our social relationships, about righting many wrongs in our government and culture that were leading us down a destructive path. This was about showing other Americans that it is now time to truly fight for our country in the battle of our lives, fight for the great American values that patriots hold dear and that made our country so great.

This was about sending a strong message that we will not bow down to Establishment puppets and lay quietly while the left aggressively shoves their Marxist ideals down our throats and turns our country into a Socialist nation. I knew it wasn't going to be easy or comfortable, but I was willing to take the slings and arrows, and walk through the fear by faith for the greater mission toward which I felt called. This was about *taking back America.*

After all, I typically live my life with the motto, "Go bold or go home."

Or, to quote a very wise man: *"I like thinking big. I always have. To me it's very simple: if you're going to be thinking anyway, you might as well think big."* — **Donald J. Trump**

The next day, I completed my campaign website and started getting everything into place. I made my decision, and I was ready.

INTRODUCTION

CHAPTER 1

WHY I RAN FOR CONGRESS AGAINST THE SPEAKER OF THE HOUSE

"You will never know how much it has cost my generation to preserve YOUR freedom. I hope you will make a good use of it."
— **John Adams**

What's Your Story? Here's Mine.

I f YOU have the courage to run for office, then, Bravo! You should be proud of yourself. If you are not considering running for office, but want to develop your bold leadership in another capacity, that's incredible too. America needs you right now.

Running for any political office is a noble feat, and it is NOT for the faint of heart. And if you're running against a career politician or famous incumbent "Goliath" like Nancy Pelosi, you will need to have balls of steel, or grow some... fast! Luckily, you will learn throughout this book how to face fear head on and develop an empowering mindset of fearlessness.

What is your reason for running for office? What is the *real* reason you're running for office?

Don't just throw your hat in the ring just to "check an item off the list" or try to get money or fame. You'll be in for a rude awakening if that's all you're going for! You really want to make sure you are running for office for the right reasons. Otherwise, your presence won't be powerful and you won't resonate with people as being authentic. It's important that you have pure intentions and understand your *Big Why*. Make sure you truly BELIEVE in the reasons you are running and have passion and fire in your soul for it. That fire inside you is the fuel that will keep you going throughout your race and then, in your career — and must remain hot. Think of each reason you have for serving our country as a firelog that you throw into that fire to build it up and intensify it. If you believe in your reasons for running for office or elevating your voice, you will command the attention of others and they will believe in you, too.

What Position or Office Will You Choose?

Congress, governor, state senate, local assembly? Maybe local school board, a councilman position, mayor of your city, or another position? Research and understand the ins and outs of each position, what are the requirements for these different types of races, and then weigh out the pros and the cons.

A good place to start is to find out who your opponents may be in each type of race, as well as the voting data from each race. Research the voting trends and what percentage of votes the candidates earned in previous elections. Once you've decided which path you want to take, and in which district, then you need to decide what a *victory* looks like for you.

Define Your Victory

What exactly are you trying to accomplish?

I had two main goals that I defined:

1. Unseating Nancy Pelosi: obviously my goal was to make it through my primary election and take her seat in Congress.

2. Raising awareness to my causes: I also had to be realistic. I knew that I was running in a tough blue district, against a deeply entrenched Democrat, in a very Democratic state. The odds were against me, and I knew it was a longshot to unseat Nancy. But I wanted to run my campaign and build my platform such that even if I lost the election, I would be a prominent political leader speaking on and raising attention to the issues I am passionate about championing. Strengthening our culture, national security, and strengthening the family unit. My goal was to continue to make an impact in these issues in America, regardless of the election results.

Use this guide to clarify your campaign "story:"

- What is your story and your background?

- How does your family, childhood, and background play a role in who you are today, as well as what causes you are passionate about championing?

- What is something unique about your background or story that you can use to give yourself an advantage?

- What were some hardships or challenges that shaped you into who you are, and influenced your views and your values?

- What is your vision for your district or state, as well as for America? How does your background and experiences make you uniquely qualified for the position you've chosen?

- What honest, realistic changes would you like to make in your district, state, and country?

- What special skills and assets could you contribute to the position?

After you've defined your big "why," your "story," and your campaign goals, then it's time to really dig into your district and get to know your area, the voters, and the people that are a part of it, very well.

★ ★ ★

As for My Story...

I wanted to fight for California, my native home. I was born and raised in California, and grew up mostly in the Bay

Area, but have family in both Northern and Southern California. When I decided to run, I had just about given up on California. I was tired of Democrats taking over the state and turning my once beautiful home into a sh*thole country. I was sick of watching them turn the major cities into "sanctuary cities" and looking the other way when illegal immigrants committed crimes, while simultaneously witnessing the growing number of homeless Americans and veterans suffering on the streets.

I wanted to fight to take back America from the corrupt Swamp because I was enraged over how aggressively and successfully they have been sabotaging Trump's America First agenda and ushering in their nefarious Marxist, globalist 2030 agenda. We have learned that there are traitors to our country everywhere, not just on the left side, but on the Republican side as well. "The Swamp" runs deep, and has tentacles in all organizations and industries. Trump has done a great job of shining the light on traitors and fake Republicans and exposing their true agenda. But he still needs more help with real patriots in office who he can trust to fight alongside him against The Swamp.

What is The Swamp?

The Swamp is a corrupt network of people in government, as well as other organizations and industries, who manipulate and control government policy, public opinion, social movements, and other things behind the scenes that impact our world. They wield real power outside the conventional checks and balances of the system. Other terms for The Swamp that are commonly used are "shadow government," "Deep State," and "The Establishment," or "the powers that be," and they are behind pretty much everything that has been going "wrong" within our country over the last 50-plus years. What is their agenda? In sum, their ultimate end-game is to overthrow our United States Constitution and sovereign, Judeo Christian-rooted nation and replace it with a godless, socialist, one-world government. The new government would have a reduced population, remove any sense of nationalism and borders, usher in a global police and military force, a big brother-style mass surveillance, and a one-world religion.

They have been the ones orchestrating the covert "Culture War" since the 1960s in order to subvert our traditional American values and replace them with secular, Marxist, globalist values. I go into more depth detailing the Cultural Marxist Revolution led by the Deep State in my previous book, *Making Love Great Again*, but this agenda isn't some kind of secret or conspiracy theory. The information can easily be confirmed with just a bit of research, and the results of their plans are evident everywhere in our society. Simply read, *The Communist Manifesto*, by Karl Marx, or look at the "45 Goals of the Communist Party"[2] which actually was read into the US congressional record in 1963, and you'll see that 90 percent of these goals already have been accomplished while the rest are well in progress. Also research The 11-Step Plan for Cultural Subversion,[3] or the Agenda 2030 for Sustainable Development,[4] or even The Green New Deal, as the globalists disguise their goals and agenda as merely innocuous "sustainable development." In order to usher in the kind of totalitarian government they want, they must replace the traditional American values of personal responsibility and maximum personal freedom with "equality for all" and dependence on the government; they need to destroy the nuclear family unit, destroy Christianity and Judeo-Christian values, replace Capitalism with Socialism, and replace patriotism, strong borders, and pride in one's country with disdain for America and borders. The fact that we have a generation of youth that believe that "America is inherently racist" and are taught to refer to themselves as "global citizens of the world" rather than American citizens is by design, not by accident. And did you really think that the surge of propaganda in the media that has been demonizing Christian principles and the traditional family unit while promoting godlessness, hedonism, and gender fluidity was just by accident?

Of course, The Swamp also have been the ones leading the covert coup to throw President Trump out of office, and they have been responsible for all of the efforts to sabotage his presidency from before his first day in office. The reason why they hate him so much and why they so desperately are trying to force him out of office? It's simple — because Trump promised to "drain The Swamp," and his pro-Constitution, America First agenda stands entirely in the way of the Deep State's agenda that they were expecting fellow Swamp member Hillary Clinton to complete.

"Our campaign represents a true existential threat — like they haven't seen before. This is not simply another four-year election. This is a crossroads in the history of our civilization that will determine whether or not we the people reclaim control over our government... This is a struggle for the survival of our nation. And this will be our last chance to save

it. This election will determine whether we are a free nation — or whether we have only the illusion of democracy, and are instead controlled by a small handful of global special interest groups rigging the system, and our system is rigged. You know it. I know it. And everyone in the world knows it." — **Donald J. Trump**

This is why I feel it's absolutely imperative to stand up and fight, *now*. We are at a crossroads in history and we simply don't have time to elect more RINOs, Swamp members, nor Communists into office.

My "big why" — I wanted to fight for America, because:

- I wanted to fight against who I call the "Head of the Snake" of The Swamp — as Nancy Pelosi has been the individual primarily leading the charge of taking my beloved country down a destructive globalist path. I wanted to fight against everything that Nancy Pelosi embodies.

- I wanted to fight for restoring the American family unit, which is being systematically dismantled by the left.

- I wanted to fight for restoring the American dream.

- I wanted to fight for President Trump's America First agenda and defend him in office against the traitors. I was so damn tired of seeing these old, low-energy, spineless representatives who stood for nothing, or even worse, became straight up sell-outs. I believe we need fresh fighters in congress with fire and energy, who are going to defend our president and fight for our country.

- I wanted to fight for free speech and our constitutional rights that I saw being chipped away.

- I wanted to fight to restore a sense of faith and shared morality that is quickly slipping away.

- I wanted to fight for our borders and national sovereignty.

- I wanted to fight to clean out corruption in our government and restore law, order, and safety in our district.

- I wanted to fight to reduce the homeless Americans and veterans suffering on the streets, taking a backseat to illegal immigrants.

One of my favorite quotes is:

"The only thing necessary for the triumph of evil is for good men to do nothing," — **Edmund Burke**

I believe God is calling everyone to stand up and fight against the evil amongst us, right now, and he needs as many good "men" (and women) as possible in His army. Because we truly *are* at War. I heard that call, I answered that call, and this is how I'm contributing to defeat evil and take back America. I've thrown my gloves off, and I'm ready for the fight.

I entered my campaign knowing the odds were against me, and it was going to be one hell of a hard journey. However, I declared right from the beginning that I wanted to judge my effort not just by the tally of votes, but by the life my words may give to the cause of a stronger America, an

America with stronger families, an America with stronger faith and values, an America that can muster the courage to solve its problems before they become a crisis, an America that remains the shining beacon of freedom for those who yearn to live free.

★ ★ ★

Why I Chose to Run Against Nancy Pelosi, in San Francisco Instead of My District at the Time (CA-33)

Well first off, I wanted to run against Nancy, because she legitimately made my blood boil with anger when she spoke. Doesn't she just make your blood simmer?? She is truly the Head of the Snake, and embodies all the evil, deception, and everything wrong in America today.

I learned the actual agenda of AOC and the radical Socialist "Squad." The Squad wants to take over our government and enforce widespread socialism, which will then lead to globalism. President Trump was in real danger. I had enough of witnessing the Squad's antics. I had enough of Democrats blocking our president's every move and making it so damn difficult for him to roll out his agenda for which more than 60 million Americans voted.

I truly believed I was the strongest candidate with a real chance to defeat Nancy. On the Democrat side, there were three Democrats running in my race against Nancy. Only one of them seemed to have a real shot though and a lot going for him that made him a formidable opponent. His name is

Shahid Buttar, and he is a far-left Pakistani, radical socialist, and Muslim, who's biggest complaint against Nancy and the Democrats is, frighteningly, that they are not far left *enough*. This is his second time running for this seat, but this time he has the endorsement of Bernie Sanders and the advantage of the entire Democratic Socialist fundraising and advertising machine, in addition to a very well-organized ground game. I think the only thing I could imagine that would be worse than Nancy Pelosi is having a radical socialist take her seat!

As for the Republican candidates in this race, there was just myself, and one other I was competing with. The honest truth is that when I originally decided to run and filed my candidacy papers, I didn't think any other Republican was running in the race. When I later found out that there was going to be a Republican, named John Dennis (who I'll refer to throughout the book as "JD"), I made a mental decision that if I got to know him and discovered he was a solid, genuine person, a strong patriot, and a viable candidate who would be the best choice to challenge Nancy, I would back down and support him. However, I learned early on that this individual was not someone I believed to be a solid patriot, and not someone who I wholeheartedly could support. This man already ran for this same seat three times over the last 10 years... and lost every time. He even ran for local supervisor in his own district, which is a heavily Republican district, and came in dead last in that race. He did not have a strong message, was not likeable nor inspiring, and fit the stereotype to a "T" of the old, arrogant, male "Establishment" Republican that had become a turn off to so many folks, especially the younger generations.

To make matters worse, JD had also recently taken over as the chairman of the local San Francisco GOP, which made the situation even stickier with both of us competing for the same District 12 Congressional seat. Prior to July, the chairman was a man named Jason Clark who everyone loved and thought of as a positive and fair leader, but Clark received an abrupt job transfer to Washington DC and had to move, giving the group less than two weeks to appoint a new chairman. JD was the only choice at the time and he was hastily voted in, even though many of the group members weren't too happy about it given the arrogant and demeaning attitude he often has. I was still willing to give him the benefit of the doubt and learn more about him, though. However, my first encounters with him confirmed my suspicions and the opinions of some other folks even further.

Early on in my campaign, I attended the annual California Republican Convention, in Indio, California, which is a huge weekend convention that thousands of Republicans attend. When I found out JD would be attending the Convention weekend as well, I was hoping to have a conversation with him while there and get a better feel for his campaign agenda and who he was as a person. However, whenever I saw him throughout the weekend, he appeared anti-social, cranky, and bitter that I was present as well and energetically working the rooms. Several times throughout the weekend, he even pulled attendees aside who had spoken with me and shamed them for talking to me! He acted like he owned the Congressional seat and was entitled to it, and without even doing any work.

What further upset me was when he made a very sexist comment about me to a male colleague, a friend I'll call "Rob," who also served in high positions in the California GOP. Throughout the weekend, Rob introduced me to many party members and showed lots of enthusiasm for my campaign. At the end of the weekend, JD found himself in one of the seminar rooms with Rob and started scolding him, saying, "You should be *ashamed* of your behavior." Rob said, "What? What behavior are you talking about?" JD continued condescendingly, "You *know* what I'm talking about, you should be ashamed!" When Rob still appeared confused, JD said, "You know the only reason why you're 'parading that girl' around to people is because you're trying to sleep with her." He added, "*I'm* the one who should be getting the endorsement, not her." He said this pretty loudly apparently in front of other delegates and professional colleagues who also happened to be in the room. It was offensive to me, and also offensive to my friend! His disdain and sexism toward me (and if you know me you know I don't throw that term around lightly) only increased over the months. I kept getting reports from sources throughout my campaign of him regularly telling other people, including my supporters that "the only reason why people are supporting DeAnna Lorraine is because she's attractive." Does he not think women can succeed in life on their merits and the only way they can get to the top is by sleeping around?

Those early impressions of the other Republican opponent, along with other things that happened later, are what kept me in the race fighting for Nancy's seat despite there being another "R" on the ticket.

I was so done with these fake Republicans, like Justin Amash and Mittens Romney, turning on President Trump and we needed to weed them out. Trump has done a great job of shining the light on traitors and RINOs — *"Republicans in Name Only"* — and exposing their true loyalty.

I could have run in my own district and saved myself a whole lot of heartache, hassle, and money, but to be honest, I wasn't *passionate* about it. The district I had lived in the last few years — California's 33rd district — was actually rather beautiful, clean, and without the tragic homelessness issue present in San Francisco. I wasn't angry enough about issues in my district to be motivated to run there. Nancy Pelosi, however, made me angry. The district of San Francisco made me angry. The suffering on the streets of San Francisco and the decline of the city over the years made me angry. When I thought about or spoke about her, I got fired up and my blood just boiled. That felt more authentic to me, because I could speak and campaign from a place of genuine passion and anger.

My RINO opponent spent a lot of time attacking me over the fact that I was moving to San Francisco to run for Congress in the district, whereas he had been a local for years and knew the district better. That may have been the case, but I found it pretty silly he obsessed about that point so much. It's not like I just flew in from Oklahoma or Alaska! I was born and raised in California and spent most of my life in the Bay Area, just about 30 minutes outside of San Francisco. He was born and raised in New Jersey. My brother Patrick had just graduated from Berkeley, which was right across the bay from the district, and my brother Emmett currently is living right in the heart of San Francisco attending law school. My parents and many of my relatives live within an hour of the city as well, and I spent a lot of time there growing up. I am *very* in-tune with the problems and issues of California, especially having lived the bulk of my life in the Democrat-run cities of Los Angeles and San Jose. Of course there was more for me to learn about the specific 12th district, but it wasn't like I was a total foreigner!

One thing I knew for sure about San Francisco that anyone can plainly see, is that it had become "ground zero" for cultural rot in America; and Nancy Pelosi is the embodiment of that rot. So, I wanted to take the fight straight to her front door. So what if I hadn't lived there for 30 years. Hey, it's 2020: time to screw the old "carpetbagger" stereotype. If you're a badass, fiery candidate, you truly care about the district, and you believe you can make a positive impact, then commit and go for it! People need to stop focusing on petty things in politics, or we'll keep electing the wrong candidates and wolves in sheep's clothing. Do we want to be petty, or do we want to be *powerful* and take back America?!

★ ★ ★

Welcome to the "Sh*tty"

I was walking around the Tenderloin district in San Francisco while freezing my butt off. It was a cold, windy September day in the city and I wasn't wearing a heavy enough jacket, so it was biting. I stepped in sh*t. Grrreat. It was most likely human sh*t, as there were no dogs around that I could see, yet dozens of homeless surrounding me. To my right was an old homeless man shooting up heroin. To my left was a crazy-eyed homeless woman screaming and cursing at me incoherently, and next to her was another man screaming about drugs. Trash and needles littered the streets, and it reeked of old garbage and urine. I hopped into my overpriced uber, to check into my overpriced, tiny, run-down motel, which had drug addicts and homeless people running around all over the halls screaming all night. As I was eating my overpriced cheeseburger and drinking my overpriced, but well-deserved glass of wine I thought, *'Do I really want to do this? Do I really want to run for Congress, and in THIS sh*t hole?'*

Did I *really* want to put myself through all this? It would be so much easier for me if I just ran back home in Redondo Beach. I knew so many people already, I had my lovely and comfortable apartment with my cat; I would save tons of money on expenses, I could leisurely walk the beautiful beachside streets in the warm weather to knock on doors. Campaigning would be a breeze just going around to many of the places and events I already frequented. Running my campaign in San Francisco would be a much greater sacrifice and would take much more out of me, because if I was going to do it, I would do it right and put my all into it.

However, the longer I thought about it, the more I realized that I *needed* to be there. Nancy Pelosi was focused on helping illegal immigrants, rather than the needs of the homeless, while struggling Americans took a backseat to the thousands crossing over from Mexico illegally. The Democratic Mayor, London Breed, was pretty much MIA. She only seemed to appear whenever there was an opportune photo opp. The other Republican candidate, JD, lived right down the street from Nancy's mansion in a very wealthy enclave of San Francisco and I honestly couldn't imagine him actually rolling up his sleeves and talking to the homeless, picking up their trash, and caring enough to make a difference. Who is going to care for these people, then? If I ran away now, then I'd be no better than Nancy Pelosi and all the other politicians who pretend to care, yet turn the other way ignoring the mess and the real Americans who need our help the most. This is why I wanted to fight for California to do my part in taking back America. I knew it was going to be a very tough journey that would test me in many ways, but I was committed. Let's do this! As I've always said, *"go bold or go home!"*

These are my reasons for throwing myself in the fire and running for Congress, what are *yours*?

I love America!

CHAPTER 2

SAVING CALIFORNIA TO SAVE AMERICA:

A DAVID & GOLIATH BATTLE

"Our confidence is not in what we have, but He who freely gave us what we have. If God's will is in your little stones, they will surely bring down giant Goliaths... but you have to make the throw!"
— **Israelmore Ayivor**

California is the case study for the rest of America. If California falls, so does the rest of America. At one time, California was a symbol of paradise that people from all over the country flocked to while others only could dream of visiting — year-round beautiful weather, beautiful gorgeous beaches, beautiful lakes, ski resorts, and beautiful, happy people. When I was younger, people from other states would envy me and consider me so lucky for being a California Girl! However, in the last few decades, the state has been totally hijacked by the radical left. California is now known for being a symbol of a pitiful riches-to-rags story; the manifestation of cultural and political failure. The images that are now associated with California are piles of needles and feces in the streets, a dying middle class, the country's highest taxes and poverty rate, and a "sanctuary" to illegal immigrants. Rather than people moving *into* California, there is now a "Calexodus" happening — thousands of middle class families and individuals are fleeing *out of* California every year to escape the horrendous conditions!

No longer the paradise that others envy, it is now the butt of all jokes and pity: "Oh you live in California? Ooh that's terrible, I feel so bad for you!" The state has become a rapidly expanding tumor that's toxic to the rest of America, spreading its disease faster than Chinese bats out of the Wuhan lab. It needs to either be cured, or cut off entirely to prevent further infectious spread.

Leftist Governor Gavin "Gruesome" Newsom and his partner in crime, Nasty Nancy Pelosi, are the puppet masters of California's destruction — although according to them, everything in the state is going just swimmingly!

To most normal people with eyes though who are living in it day in and day out, Los Angeles and San Francisco have undoubtedly become the worst cities in the state, and I've been determined to make sure the rest of America did NOT turn into the worst parts of San Francisco. I felt compelled to take the fight for our nation's soul and our country's future directly to the front lines.

Study Your Area

I think being an outsider to the city actually gave me an advantage in many ways, even though my RINO opponent attacked me heavily for it, because I approached the situation from a "documentarian" point of view. People who have lived in San Francisco for decades already were numb to most of the atrocities, whereas I came in with a fresh set of eyes, like an auditor examining what's broken and set on determining how it can be improved.

But still, if I wanted to be able to speak confidently about the district in the media, propose solutions to the needs of constituents, and relate to them on a level that would earn their votes, I knew I would need to learn as much as I could about the district. I wanted to become an expert in the things that mattered to them. I wanted to dive in, get dirty, and really get to know the area as much as possible. So, I got to know the real people. I talked to the locals and interviewed them. I talked to the tourists. I hung out with and interviewed the homeless and panhandlers circling the dirty and dangerous neighborhoods. I had long conversations with residents walking their dogs, with people sitting on bus stops and riding the BART metro trains. I got to know the laws, the latest news, and new legislation coming down the pipe. And, most of all, I listened, listened, and then listened some more.

I truly was shocked to see the level of gross negligence and decay in some parts of San Francisco. Many neighborhoods resembled Third World country conditions, and the current representatives didn't seem to care a bit. While walking around I saw packs of homeless suffering on the streets, being left there to starve and rot. Dozens of people strung out on drugs and openly doing or exchanging drugs right out there in the open. People shooting up with dirty needles, smoking crack or marijuana and getting drunk to pass the time away. I honestly didn't even know if many of the people I passed were dead or alive because they were so lifeless or strung out. It's truly heartbreaking. There were a lot of feces in the streets and trash thrown about everywhere — yet the local law enforcement didn't seem to have anything under control.

Walking around those areas at night, especially as a woman, is even scarier. Each time I had to walk a street or two at night to get to a destination, I held my breath, said a little prayer, and felt like I cheated death once I made it to my destination alive. What really ruffled my feathers is that even amidst such unruly and unsafe conditions, Nancy and the Squad kept pushing to have our borders wide open with illegal immigrants flooding through, causing our own backyards to be more dangerous and more crime-ridden than ever. Meanwhile these elite politicians are protected by guns, gate-guarded mansions, and bodyguards, yet they want *us little people* to be defenseless and disarmed as they keep pushing for "greater gun control."

In October of 2019, the Board of Supervisors in San Francisco even had the audacity to label the NRA a National Terrorist Organization! Yet in the same breath the same Democrats claimed that *actual* domestic terrorists, Antifa, were merely "peaceful protesters" who meant no harm.

That's the Democratic mode of operation: jack up the crime and chaos, and disarm the citizens affected by it. What does that say about Nancy and Democratic concern for America's well-being? It should tell normal, rational people everything they need to know. However, I soon realized I wasn't dealing with "normal, rational" people and I had a long road ahead of me of shaking up and waking up the masses of heavily indoctrinated minds.

Why have these conditions been allowed to manifest? How did it even become so bad?

When I continued to explore deeper, I easily connected the Democrat dots and began to understand how California and the district of San Francisco became what they are today. All roads to destruction lead to Democrats!

A review of various aspects of life in California make obvious the failure of Democratic rule:

- Forty percent of California's population lives near poverty.

- California has among the highest taxes in the country, highest priced housing, and highest gas prices in the country.

- California is home to more undocumented immigrants than any other state. In late 2017, Governor Jerry Brown made California a "sanctuary state" by signing California Sanctuary Law SB54. This means the state prohibits law enforcement agents from asking about a person's immigration status or participating in any program that uses them as immigration agents.

- In 2019, California went a step further and became the first state to offer taxpayer-funded health benefits to young adults living in the country illegally — "in order to improve the health of immigrants." Gavin Newsom signed this bill into law, which makes low-income adults age 25 and younger eligible for the state's Medicaid program — regardless of their immigration status. The plan covers about 90,000 people — and costs taxpayers $98 million.[5] Newsom and his Democratic legislative leaders say they plan to expand coverage even further to more adults in the years to come.

- Most expensive place to live while surrounded by crap: San Francisco has seen complaints of human waste on public streets and sidewalks skyrocket by 400 percent in the last decade — all on Nancy Pelosi's watch. So, the same Democratic government that seeks to provide a "sanctuary" and every need for illegal immigrants has clearly failed to provide the most basic level of cleanliness and decency for residents.

- As if that's not bad enough, I discovered that in 2018, California Democratic leaders thought it would be a great idea to pass SB 239, which made it no longer a felony in California to *knowingly expose* someone to HIV with the intent of transmitting the virus. Gov Jerry Brown *decriminalized* this heinous act, lowering it from a felony to a misdemeanor with a maximum of six months jail time, as well as eliminating the penalty for knowingly donating HIV-infected blood. Why? Because the Democrats feared it would stigmatize people living with HIV and "hurt their feelings." How does this make any sense?? Can anyone please explain to me how that makes Californians safer and healthier??

- Despite pouring $300 million dollars the past year into *the homelessness problem*, the number of homeless individuals living on the streets in San Francisco alone has risen 17 percent in the past year — now up to nearly 10,000 just in San Francisco, and more than 151,000 homeless individuals in the state of California — according to the U.S. Department of Housing and Urban Development from the latest tally (2020)[6].

I realized that the entire homelessness epidemic in California is a result of Democratic policies. It was Democrats who pushed for policies to empty the jails and prisons of "nonviolent" offenders. It was Democrats who successfully pushed for laws that downgraded property and drug crimes, such as the insidious Proposition 47, passed in 2016. It was Democrats who successfully pushed for laws that made housing prohibitively expensive to those who were marginally employed. It was Democrats who built shelters at ludicrous costs in the middle of stable neighborhoods, putting zero behavioral requirements on those being sheltered (no sobriety requirement, no curfew, no background checks).

Did they really think that would turn out well?

You would think... you would THINK that maybe California's leaders might put more attention into helping the middle class stay in California and resolving the growing homelessness or crime problem. Instead, they spend all their time talking about xenophobia, transphobia, gender issues, banning straws, and floating Baby Trump blimps to mock President Trump.

California Democrats like to do everything they can to be the leader in the ludicrous race to corrupt the minds and values of every man, woman, worker, and child with their increasingly insidious laws and policies. They completely perverted our children through the education system by systematically removing Christian values and American ideals from schools, while pushing Marxist propaganda like increasingly earlier Sex Ed, Draq Queen Story Hour, and teaching kindergarteners to experiment with different genders.

And the heinous and backwards priorities of California Democratic leaders continued to shock me. In October 2019, the mayor of San Francisco, London Breed, pushed a radical new measure that *forbid* employees of San Francisco to take work trips or do business with companies in any state (22 of them) that have "restrictive abortion laws," like the "fetal heartbeat laws." Because of course, according to these Democratic dictators, daring to believe that life is sacred instead of "abortion anytime on-demand" is "wrongthink," and must be punished!

Mayor Breed proudly declared, "Every day in this country, women's reproductive rights are threatened, and we have to fight back. Just as we restricted spending with states that have laws that discriminate against LGBTQ people, we are standing up against states that put women's health at risk and that are actively working to limit reproductive freedoms."[7]

WHAT? Not only is this totally Orwellian straight out of *1984*, but it also clearly discriminates against Christians and anyone believing in the sanctity of life. The message from San

Francisco Communist leadership is loud and clear: "you MUST believe and think exactly how we think, or else we will force you to." It's scary, it's a slippery slope and these kinds of totalitarian policies will sweep over the rest of the country, too, if people like you and me stay quiet and don't step up to stop this madness.

How About the New Assembly Bill 5?

You also would *think* that California's ruling Democratic Party might be concerned about keeping as many jobs as possible in the state, right? Alas, this is far too much common sense for the illogical left!

With Assembly Bill 5, passed in 2020, Democrat lawmakers not only came up with a solution for which there is no problem, they created hardships for workers where there were none before. Instead of helping the workers, Assembly Bill 5 actually created an employment nightmare, causing issues for many. Companies most impacted by the Bill's restrictions are Uber, Lyft, private contractors, and construction companies. Rather than create new opportunities, many have lost employment opportunities and they are justifiably furious.

This AB 5 Bill was of course championed by Governor Newsom — who, frighteningly, wants to be our president in the near future.

If Nancy and these leaders spent half as much time focusing on fixing the REAL issues that *real* Americans are facing, rather than on identity politics, giving free healthcare to illegal immigrants, or which gender pronouns we should use, we might actually make real progress. But of course they do not, and they will not, because their agenda is to *intentionally* wipe out the middle class, create chaos, and then pretend to be the "saviors" and usher in their own socialist "solution" to that chaos. The "solution," of course, which would result in us Americans dependent on big government and no longer a free and sovereign people.

I could go on and on about the failures of Democratic leadership decimating my home state, but the most recent local election in San Francisco pretty much sums up the mental illness of Californians and gave a chilling preview of where the state is headed: in the November local election, the people of San Francisco cast their vote and overwhelmingly made their choice for their new Attorney General — the incredible, talented Chesa Boudin! Yes, the man who — get this — is *literally* a Communist and whose parents were literally in a radical, left-wing domestic terrorist organization called the *Weather Underground,* with the political mission of fueling a revolution "to overthrow American imperialism and form a classless, Communist world." They were thrown in prison when Boudin was a child for inciting violence, blowing up government buildings, and *murdering police officers.*[8] YOU JUST CAN'T MAKE THIS STUFF UP!

And how did the openly cop-hating Boudin win the hearts of San Franciscans enough to get elected? Why, on his promises to further decriminalize gang activity and "quality of life crimes," which included defecating and urinating on the streets, offering or soliciting sex, public camping, and theft, among a long list of other things. San Francisco voters assessed all of their current problems and feces they're swimming in and said, "Yes, give me more crime! More trash!

Give me full-blown communism! Sounds great, bring it on!" I just can't. You'd think this was satire, but it is an unfortunate reality for us California residents.

If hearing this causes you to pull your hair out and scream, you're not alone. My hair is significantly thinner after my experience running for Congress in this Liberal twilight zone. *Remember*, these Democratic leaders want to run our entire country with the same policies that California has put in place. Visualize these same Third World-esque conditions in every city and county in your own beautiful state. *That* is what we have in our near future if we continue to have far-left, Communist Democrats elected and why it's *so* important that more of us step up to stop them.

Once I had a better understanding of the dire situation on the local and state level and what I was really up against — while making me want to punch a few things — only strengthened my will to fight for California and solidified my commitment to defeat the Queen of this dystopian dream, Nancy Pelosi. I simply could not allow the rest of America to turn into her maniacal Socialism experiment. We have a LOT at stake in San Francisco. The city is at the brink of falling completely to socialism if my radical Socialist opponent Shahid Buttar were to win in November. We cannot just wave the white flag of surrender as the left turns each beautiful state — and then the country — into Venezuela.

Did I have all the answers? No. Did I have a political science degree? No. Did I know everything there is to know about how Congress works? Definitely not. But I'm sharp, a quick study, and determined to learn everything I needed to be successful once elected.

The most important credentials I do have are absolute love and loyalty to our country, determination, and a blazing, fiery fighting spirit. We need badass warriors leading our country who will fight for not only their state, but for America; fight to protect our Constitution and defend our values and way of life. One warrior at a time, one city at a time, one state at a time, we must fight to take our country back. Yes it *was* a David & Goliath battle, but remember who won in the end? These points became part of my campaign "Battle Song."

CHAPTER 3

BUILD A WINNING CAMPAIGN BRAND

"If everyone fought for their own convictions, there would be no war."
— **Leo Tolstoy**

Build Your Platform and Brand So it Lives On, Regardless of the Election Outcome

A fter you've defined your campaign story and overall goals, it's time to think about your campaign platform and brand. Whether you're looking to win support for an issue, impact policy, or inspire donors to take action and give, in order to have a winning campaign, it's important to take the time to thoughtfully and strategically plan it out.

What is Your Campaign Platform?

Your campaign platform is like the mission statement of a company that tells people what you're all about, what you stand for, as well as your top goals or issues that you are championing.

What do you stand for? How will you solve your target market's greatest needs and concerns? Why should people get behind you, donate to you, defend you, volunteer for you?

Your campaign platform should answer those questions and inspire people to get behind you, as well as volunteer, rally, donate, and vote for you! Your campaign platform should align well with your "story." Your "brand" encompasses everything: your story, platform, image, logo, slogan, and messaging.

Defining Your Core Issues

As you're developing your campaign platform, the first thing you want to do is make a list of the issues about which you have strong and passionate views — list everything in your heart. Then, narrow those down to three main issues, which will become the core issues that define your campaign and that you'll address frequently, whether on your campaign trail or in your activism.

It's ideal if these are issues to which you are personally and emotionally connected, so you can truly speak from the heart. If a woman's son was killed by an illegal immigrant, then fixing the immigration system and building the wall would probably be a core campaign issue for her. Or maybe you had an experience where a gun saved your life in a bad situation, so championing the second amendment might be a main issue for you.

For me, repairing the broken family unit, which included solving the "Boy Crisis" and reducing fatherless homes, was my most important issue. It's something I've always been passionate about, because I wanted everyone else to have the whole and complete family that I didn't always have growing up. I also realized through working closely with people and learning more about their personal lives in my coaching practice and in writing my previous book, that most of the problems we have in our country today can be attributed to the breakdown of the American family unit. For instance, while researching for my first book, I learned that children who grow up in single-parent families are more likely to have behavioral and mental-health problems, perform poorly in schools, drop out of school, attempt suicide, commit crimes, end up in juvenile hall and prisons, and be late in life to join the workforce.[1] Also, too many boys who grow up without a present father never learn how to be a man and end up drifting through life weak, lost, and without a purpose — becoming angry or apathetic and a drain on the community instead of an asset. And in a time when we've seen dozens of mass shootings, it was very relevant for me to draw attention to the fact that nearly all of the mass shooters are boys who have come from fatherless homes. NO politician seemed to want to talk about this — and certainly not Nancy Pelosi — so I believed it was time to have an honest national discussion about the current state of the American family unit and how we can restore it.

Another core issue for me is immigration. I see immigration, and the war around it, as another crux of many of the issues I champion. Since California is a sanctuary state and San Francisco a sanctuary city, these policies have led to much of the crime, lawlessness, debt, drugs, human trafficking, and problems in the school system. I also believe having strong borders is not only practical and wise, but essential, symbolically: no sovereign country can long remain sovereign absent secure borders, and a country that cannot control its borders *cannot control its destiny.* In order to preserve our way of life, our traditions, our safety, and our spirit of American exceptionalism, we *need* to have strong borders.

Laura Loomer, a super badass warrior and friend of mine who currently is running in Florida's 21st congressional district against Lois Frankel, is a stellar example of having your story align with your platform. She rose to fame with her bold and truthful journalistic work, which led her to be labeled "dangerous" by the left and became the "most banned person on the Internet" when the Big Tech mafia removed her from every social media platform, and even Uber, Lyft, and payment platforms. So, she has been fighting to preserve free speech and breaking up Big Tech as the main issues of her platform — and we can trust that without a doubt, she will do everything in her power to deliver on her promises, if elected, since she has been so personally impacted by these issues.

My friend Dalia al-Aqidi is another badass congressional candidate who is running against the inflammatory Ilhan Omar, in Minnesota's 5th congressional district. Like Omar, al-Aqidi is also a Muslim refugee who sought a better life in America. However, unlike Omar, she is proud of our nation and works every day to fulfill the oath she made when she became a citizen. My friend, al-Aqidi, has seen the consequences of Omar's version of an ideal government — she's seen the kind of hatred it inspires and what it has done to the Middle East. That's why al-Aqidi felt that it was her responsibility to stop her — to stop the widening rift among

Americans and instead unite our country under the values for which she immigrated here. It makes sense then, that she made fighting for legal immigration and preserving the Constitution the main focus of her campaign.

So, what issues are you passionate about? Spend quality time soul-searching and recording answers to these questions. Brainstorm and talk this through with trusted friends and your campaign team. The more personal your campaign, the better, because the more people will identify with you and your cause. People rally behind people they like and trust. The reason they trust them is because they truly feel confident that this person will follow through on the things that they're promising to do or change. How can people tell when politicians seem like they would truly deliver on their promises or they're just going to sell them a bill of goods and let them down in the end? When someone has a personal connection to an issue, they are personally invested in achieving it. Making big campaign promises and goals will appear empty if they aren't backed by personal connection, nor will it tug on anyone's heartstrings and engage their emotions. Remember this: emotions are compelling and very effective. Emotions win over dry facts and data any day. Just look how effective Liberals are at this. This is one area where we actually can learn from them!

These are questions you'll want to answer or hire a consultant to help guide you through the answers:

- What are you passionate about?

- In which areas or topics would you like to see positive change for your district? The country?

- What's your vision for the future of your district? The country?

- Know your opponents and their positions: what issues are your opponents championing? What are the weaknesses you see in their platform, policies, and/or positions? Where are opportunities for you to be unique and stand out?

Evaluate the Current Political Climate

Evaluate the current political climate on both the national level, and the local level, if you are running for office to represent a certain district. Your campaign should be tailored and customized to the current climate and events. Since Nancy Pelosi is so visible every day as the Speaker of the House, most people think of her as more of a national figurehead, influencing decisions nationally, instead of just locally in the little 12th District of San Francisco. And since she is so horrendous and divisive, people from all over the country either love her, or despise her. Either way, she incites an emotional reaction from people. So, I needed to make some of my campaign and platform issues things that resonated with my target demographic, both locally and nationally, since national support is important in building your support, increasing fundraising, earning media, and increasing your visibility. During my congressional run, the issues that were most pressing in the political climate were impeachment and immigration. So, I used those hot button issues to create my platform and messaging.

Our current president ultimately won the election for a number of reasons, but one very important reason being: he understood the *mood* of the current political and cultural climate, and capitalized on it. He understood what issues were *really important* to everyday Americans, and made those his core issues of his campaign. He talked about these issues and concerns with such passion and realness that it actually felt like he was in our heads, saying exactly what we were personally thinking, but too afraid to say publicly.

Millions of Americans were sick and tired of a president who seemed to be destroying America, annihilating our sense of patriotism, our American traditions, and way of life. We were tired of a president who constantly apologized for America and made us feel that the country is "racist" and something of which we should be ashamed! We were hungry for a president who demonstrated bold leadership and toughness; who conveyed a real passion to restore America to greatness and revive the American spirit. Trump's campaign slogan, "Make America Great Again," was exceptional. His campaign branding: the red MAGA hats, the "Proud to be an American" song that played anytime he appeared, his unabashed patriotism and display of American flags, and his many catchphrases, like "build the wall" and "jobs, not mobs," and "lock her up," lit a fire in people's hearts that was infectious. And, it is still burning very hot today.

This year, I predict President Trump will win again by a landslide. Well, the only way he will lose is if the Democrats cheat hard enough, which is a whole other issue I'll get to later. But just look at Sleepy, Creepy Joe Biden's messaging compared to Trump's, and what do you notice? Even his messaging and brand is bland and "sleepy." Biden has no consistent (or coherent), strong message, and he is all over the place! His main message is: *"Trump is bad. And you are bad for supporting him!"*

Have the Democrats not learned *anything* from Hillary's humiliating campaign?? He has even asked the public on his social media platforms what his campaign messaging and "buzzwords" should be that he should use. What is this, amateur hour?! That's like putting a sign on your forehead that reads "I have no idea what you care about and what you're concerned with, so help me out." And then to top it off, he sets off on a creepy bus tour across the US with the slogan, "No Malarky!" This slogan conveys literally nothing in the way of information or themes while reminding everyone of his weaknesses — he is very old, out of touch, and acts like a straight clown! If you go to his website or hear him talk, you do not get any feel for what he supports and what kind of future we would have if he were elected. And since he is so afraid to offend people and he's been trained like a good little monkey to be "politically correct," he panders to women, blacks, and other minority groups, so obviously that it is cringy to watch. There is just no comparison with Sleepy Joe's campaign platform, messaging, and overall brand with President Trump's. Frankly, all of the Democrats who were participating in the Clown Show this year, I mean running for president, had terrible, bland, pandering messages that made most of us gag. You can learn a lot from all of these candidates about what to do and what not to do when it comes to understanding the current political climate, and crafting your platform, messaging, and brand.

Some questions to help you evaluate your current political climate:

- What are the hot button topics and issues in the news right now with which Americans are very concerned? Choosing a hot button issue is ideal especially if your main opponent has a different (and worse) stance on it than you.

- When you've chosen an issue, what is the current conversation and "mood" around your issue?
- What's the current status of your issue? And what would be your ideal outcome or solution for it?
- What is your opposition's position on this issue?
- Who else is working on this issue?

- What current events or opportunities can you use to your advantage to highlight this issue?

Research Local District and Voter Issues

As much as it is important to be in tune with the national hot button issues and sentiment of your target demographic, it is also important to become well-versed in the local issues, especially if you are running a race against someone who isn't very nationally well-known. One of the first things you should do early in your campaign is find out the local voter demographics (age, gender, income, etc.) as well as trends in their voting history. Information on past elections and voter demographics can be found on the website of your state, county, city, or town, as well as the census.gov website. Along with the hard voter data, you also need to become familiar with local issues and grievances within the government, so you can customize your campaign even further to have it resonate with your local voters — as those are ultimately the people who will elect you, or not! Follow current local and state government officials on social media, and pay attention to how those officials react to certain issues and news events. Attend local political meetings, town halls, and events to get involved in the current conversations. Familiarize yourself with the platforms of your opponents who are running for your seat, along with candidates from previous elections. How effective were they in reaching out to the voters? Watch and read the local news, and peruse websites like votesmart.org to help familiarize yourself with current political issues, as well as provide information on elected officials in your area. Knowing the incumbent's stances, and those of your potential competitors, will help you finalize your platform and core issues, as well as your strategies for reaching out to and influencing voters. You may be passionate about being pro-life and reducing abortion for instance, but if it's not really a hot button issue nationally or in your local district, then you may not want to make that one of your core issues in your platform. Of course, talk to and listen to the people of the district. Have as many conversations as possible, ask them questions, and listen, listen, listen. Ideally your views are similar to those of your constituents and you can run on a platform that aligns the two.

Some questions to ask locals in your district:

- What are your biggest concerns right now? What local issues are not being handled well and what would you want to be done differently?

- How do you feel the current representatives (president, congressperson, mayor, etc.) are doing right now? What would you want them to do differently or better?

- What is your stance on XYZ issue?

Personally, my three original core issues were: the family unit, immigration, and protecting free speech. However, once I really dove in and got to know the district better and talked to the people to find out what were the most pressing issues for them, I realized that fixing the homelessness crisis was a top priority for most of the residents in the city and it really needed to be one of my core issues.

After you've become attuned to the current political climate, and researched national issues, local issues, and voter demographics, it's time to finalize your campaign platform and core issues. Definitely have your campaign advisors and team help you to customize and finalize your campaign platform.

Talking to the homeless on the streets of San Francisco.

The following were my top three campaign goals; choose your top three issues:

1. Immigration: ensure our nation remains a sovereign nation by tightening our immigration system and building that wall!

2. Homelessness: focus on getting the homeless and unemployed off the streets, off government dependencies, into jobs, and helping to restore their dignity.

3. The family unit: focus on strengthening the American family, marriage, and the relationship between men and women, because strong families equal a strong America.

Chart Your Course to Victory

With your rockstar campaign team, lay out your milestones that you must hit on your way to reach your campaign goals. Ideally, these steps should build off each other and indicate that your campaign is gaining momentum.

Create a Winning and Memorable Logo, Messaging, and Website

Running a campaign or championing a cause is really the same as creating a winning business and brand image: your presentation, image, colors, tagline, logo, and brand "story" all play a pivotal role in your business being a huge success where you're selling like hotcakes, or it could be a huge flop.

Is the product packaged well? Is it resonating with people? Is it evoking their emotions and senses? Do they trust it? Do they trust the seller? Is it registering with them that this is something they both want and *need* or must have?! How is it unique from competing options?

Once you've identified your campaign platform and the core issues you want to champion, then it's time to create your campaign slogan and logo. Marketing yourself as the leading candidate requires a captivating slogan and recognizable campaign logo. Voters gravitate towards those they recognize, so creating a badass identifiable campaign brand will grow your following and support faster. Your campaign slogan should reflect your ideals and mission. In order to create a memorable slogan, it must evoke an emotional response with voters.

To accomplish this, ask the following questions:

- ❏ Who is your target audience?
- ❏ What values or results are important to them?
- ❏ What phrase represents you, your values, and/or your campaign's core issues?
- ❏ What are a few words that epitomize the mission for which you're fighting or the results your voters want in their future?

The message is important. The messenger, and the packaging of that messenger are *very* important. If you're planning on running for office, this is why you should allow yourself time to thoroughly complete this vitally important planning stage.

Your logo should include your name, the position you're seeking, and your slogan, with no more than three colors. There should be something recognizable and unique about your logo. If it's too busy or includes too much text, it can overwhelm people and not resonate nor stick in their minds. Think of how it will look on a T-shirt, business card, or campaign brochure. Simple logos that convey your campaign message will become recognizable as you advertise during the campaign.

I spent many days trying to determine the perfect tagline and logo. I had a huge list of words and phrases that represented my campaign and mission. After going back and forth a lot, I finally decided on one. It seemed simple enough, but I just couldn't think of any other three words that better embodied the three things I always talked about that I valued so much, which were so important for our country to truly become "great" again:

Faith, Family, and Patriotism: God, Family, and Country.

I also remembered certain quotes from our Founding Fathers and other instrumental American leaders:

> *"Only a virtuous people are capable of freedom. As nations become more corrupt and vicious, they have more need of masters."* — **Benjamin Franklin**

> *"Our Constitution was made only for a moral and religious People. It is wholly inadequate to the government of any other."* — **John Adams**

Yep, that was it. A lot of folks told me I should have something more "California" specific or "San Francisco" specific. However, the race I was running in and Nancy Pelosi herself, was a race that is much bigger than just the 12th District. She is a national figurehead who has national disdain, making changes on a national level. What was I going to have my slogan be, *"Stop sh*tting on San Francisco?"* or *"Make San Francisco less trashy and less sh*tty again?"* Somehow those didn't have the right ring to them. So, God, Family, Country it was. Short and to the point.

Some people, including Republicans, told me it was "too bold" to have the word "God" in my slogan and I'd be pissing off the atheists or Liberals. Well the atheists could shove it as far as I'm concerned, because I'm not really targeting atheists anyhow. "But, San Francisco is so secular," they said. Welp, if any city needed God, family, and patriotism the most, it was certainly San Francisco, which has become the epicenter of spiritual decay in America, especially under *Nasty* Pelosi's reign. In fact, that city needs to be showered long and hard in Holy Water.

Turn Your Weaknesses into Assets

When it came to crafting my message, I struggled a bit at first. I looked at the backgrounds and resumes of many other political figures, which were so extensive and intimidating. I did not go to an Ivy League university like Harvard or Yale. I did not have an impressive master's or doctorate degree. I went to a California State University and proudly earned my bachelor's degree, but I felt it dwarfed in comparison. I didn't come from a political pedigree, didn't study political science at school, never ran for office before, or even worked on any political campaigns. I was just an ordinary American, who worked at a corporate job out of college, then quit to start my own business in a field about which I was passionate. I wrote a book, studied social psychology, and had a YouTube channel. How was I going to sound impressive? Well, I realized that I could either "sound" impressive on paper or *be* impressive with my words and actions.

After talking to one of my consultants, I realized that what I perceived as my weaknesses actually could be *repositioned* as my strengths. Yes, I might be considered just an "ordinary" American — but I was doing bold, extraordinary things and going way out of my comfort zone, because I care so damn much about this country that I felt called to fight in a big way. President Trump set the new standard for this new wave of leaders to emerge who didn't necessarily come from hefty political backgrounds where they were raised and groomed to be politicians. One of the huge reasons we love him so much is BECAUSE of this fact, that he is *one of us* — he's real, he's unscripted and unpolished, he has been in the trenches with us dealing with the real problems affecting Americans. Mitt Romney or Jeb Bush seem so fake and "puppet-like" now, so unrelatable when you compare them with our Trump.

He turned his weakness into a strength. So, I did the same. AOC lowered the bar even further by shocking the hell out of everyone and winning her race over the deeply entrenched Establishment incumbent and she was just a bartender prior to running for office.

Nancy Pelosi, Mitt Romney, Joseph Crowley (defeated by AOC), and my opponent — they all represent the "Old Guard" of politicians.

However, it's time to be out with old, in with the new and *bold.*

It's 2020: welcome to the *New School* of government where real Americans who are relatable and have a real heart for this country and the concerns for the American people are now welcomed.

The honest truth is, it was never my goal in life to become a politician. I'm *not* a "seasoned politician" who's been out of touch sitting in a gate-guarded mansion the last 30 years. However, I AM a passionate and angry American, who's been right here in the trenches *with* my fellow Americans. As I said earlier, I care so damn much about this country that I will not let it go down without a fight.

Then there was the factor of my young age. Nancy Pelosi is in her 70s, my RINO opponent is in his 60s, *then me, half their ages.* I was worried I could be accused of not having enough experience or wisdom to do the job, but I also turned that into my advantage: Nancy was old and senile; my opponent was old and lethargic; and I am a fresh, bold new voice, and rising star, full of energy with innovative ideas. Nancy had been in Congress for more than 30 years, since I was a toddler. That's not an asset, that's a problem! My other Republican opponent had run for office already four times over the last decade. He lost horribly every time, so clearly this means something is not working for him and voters simply don't find him to be a strong enough or a likeable candidate to get him to the finish line!

As I always said during my stump speeches, I may not have Nancy's old age, but I've got some things she doesn't. Let's start with energy, honesty, and (sane) fresh ideas that work! Boom.

Create Your "Messaging Matrix" for Maximum Impact

Once you've crafted your campaign platform and slogan, you should create what I call a messaging matrix — a document that has catchy soundbites, talking points, and catchphrases that you will use throughout your campaign, along with your positions on key issues. You will eventually memorize these, and have your campaign team members and volunteers do the same, as it will help keep you sounding sharp, consistent, and recognizable. You become memorable by repeating the same soundbites and stances on certain issues. You want people to associate your name immediately with the issues you support, what you're all about, immediately have a positive image of you, and know your catchphrases.

Create Your "Campaign Speech"

Your campaign speech — also called a "stump speech" — is a speech that you will give all throughout your campaign, either verbatim or customized versions of it to better fit the specific event or group to whom you're speaking. Your speech should include all your best soundbites and talking points, as well as the reasons you are running for this position, the difference you are going to make, if elected, and the core issues that you are championing. Your speech should leave people feeling empowered, hopeful, excited, and inspired. It should touch their hearts, and compel them to want to volunteer for you, support you, and donate to you!

Other Action Items:

- ❏ Secure professional photos and a campaign video ad.
- ❏ Start writing your campaign kick-off speech.

**Make sure that you're a part of my growing community of fearless patriots as we fight together in the war of our lives to take back America. Join my Inner Circle email list and Telegram group—this is our "safe space" to freely communicate about all of these issues, organize, mobile rallies and other important actions that we need to take to fight back & take back America: Deannalorraine.com/inner-circle

Also be sure you subscribe to my Podcast, **Taking Back America!** I broadcast every Tuesday, Wednesday & Thursday from **YouTube**, **Periscope, iTunes,** and other channels and I keep you updated on the latest breaking news *as well as my upcoming events.*

YouTube.com/c/DeAnnaLorraine

Twitter.com/DeAnna4Congress

CHAPTER 4

GRAB YOUR SPONGES, BLEACH, AND SCRUB A DUB AWAY!

"People think computers will keep them from making mistakes. They're wrong. With computers you make mistakes faster."
— **Adam Osborne**

Y ou are now running for public office. If you make all the right moves, you may actually BE in office next year! Think like a winner. Act like a winner. Talk like a winner.

So, as a winner and a high-profile leader, you have to assume that EVERYTHING you have said in the past, every post you have made, every message sent may now be under a microscope and read by thousands of people. Even very innocent-seeming posts could come back to haunt you. If someone wants to find dirt on you, they won't stop at anything to make it happen. It's time to scrub your social media accounts.

The last thing you want is to be sitting in office and have everything for which you've worked so hard topple to the ground, because some unsavory picture or post that you made years ago was unearthed by social media "snarchaeologists."

We are now, sadly and thanks to the left, living in "cancel culture." We've seen too many public figures get swiftly cancelled and killed off, simply because of one picture. One bad joke. One comment that wasn't even racist. Don't let this happen to you.

Something you said even years prior that may have been in jest, in a moment of passion or anger can be misinterpreted or distorted to create a narrative about you that may be totally false. When I first decided to run, I made a decision that I had nothing to hide, because I am a good person, I've never committed any crimes and I wanted to be totally transparent and authentic. Yikes, was I ever mistaken?!

Certain people from my opponent's camp found a few videos and quotes I made years ago and had a field day with them. You don't want something minor and irrelevant to become the main focus of your campaign and distract people from your message and merits. I had to fight this false information the whole time during my campaign, and it was miserable.

My previous occupation was as a relationship and personal development coach. I started my business at the ripe old age of 24 when I had enough with the corporate world. I decided I wanted to be my own boss and do what I was passionate about instead of working for someone else doing a job that didn't meaningfully impact the world. In a short amount of time, I became a leading figurehead in that industry and had a popular YouTube channel sharing a broad spectrum of advice videos that covered everything from communication skills to social anxiety, to confidence-building strategies, to relationships and dating. The book that I wrote and published documented that "red-pilled" journey of how I came to realize that liberalism and radical feminism have led to the destruction of our relationships, the family unit, and our culture, and I illustrated how the political, cultural and personal are all interconnected and under attack by the left.

Prior to the start of my campaign, I felt it best to remove many of these videos and online material on these topics to avoid the risk of the material being misconstrued and used as weapons to smear me. However, some people still dug up some things, and used them accordingly.

One certain media blogger who had it out for me due to his alliance with my opponent somehow discovered a podcast from 2009, entitled "Halloween special!" This particular episode included a guest who was giving tips on "fantasy for Halloween." It was an innocuous and silly episode, but if you are a TV host or podcaster you obviously have to have entertaining guests and topics and tie things into holidays, otherwise no one will listen. Based on this one podcast episode though, the blogger wrote an article entitled something along the lines of, "Omg, DeAnna Lorraine is a freak! Look at this podcast from 2009. This is why you need to vote for John Dennis instead!" Eh, whatever, it was more than 10 years ago and taken totally out of context! However, in the political world, people just love to run their mouths because they have nothing better to do, so it just gave my haters extra ammo to use against me. Luckily, nothing they dug up about me was really that incriminating, but you definitely need to consider everything posted in the public domain that could be misconstrued.

Before you announce that you're going to run for office is when you want to do a major clean up. Think hard and make a list. Do your friends have anything on their social media accounts: Instagram, Facebook, Twitter, Snapchat, or any other online account or website that you wouldn't want the world to see? What about Tinder, online dating sites, hmmm? Clean up all those accounts or better yet, remove the profiles! What about clients, former clients, or other business associates? Is there anyone who could be disgruntled or any unresolved situation? Be prepared for anything to come back at you.

Now is a Good Time to Send Everyone You Know Non-Disclosure Agreements (NDAs)

It may seem silly to you now, but you'll thank me later for this advice. You don't want to be worrying about someone from your past or present coming out with some crazy story about you or leaking something that the media can distort. Social media can be your best friend, but also your greatest enemy. Do the work now and reap the rewards later.

Get Your House in Order

Before announcing your run is the best time to "get your house in order." Complete with integrity anything that needs resolution, otherwise those may end up becoming your worst trolls. Are there any other 'skeletons' in your closet? If so, either clean them up, resolve them, or be prepared with your positions and statements on them in case you're ever asked about any of those issues at some point. You may not be able to resolve every issue, but you should at least be prepared and able to answer for them so you won't be caught off guard.

As for your finances, you should have as much money saved as possible, ideally at least three months rent or expenses saved, before you start your campaign. You may have to dip into your own personal money for a bit in the beginning until your fundraising really takes off, which is why you should not be completely scrapped for cash when you start your run.

Action Items:

- ❑ Look through all your social media accounts and online photo albums. Go all the way back. Scrub any posts with strong opinions or comments that may possibly be construed as racist, sexist, or homophobic.

- ❑ Scrub comments, pictures, and videos related to sex, partying, or anything at all that may be in opposition to your platform and values that you are championing?

- ❑ Delete any photobuckets, Flikka, Pinterest, or old online photo albums.

- ❑ Delete photos and videos from your phone, emails, and iCloud that you wouldn't want out there in case someone "came upon it," aka hacked into it. Don't believe me? Oh read on, dear naive friend. You're playing with the big dogs now.

❏ Have ex-partners, ex-professional clients, friends, neighbors, and family members sign NDAs.

❏ Resolve issues with friends, co-workers, colleagues, family members, anyone with potential issues. Be as bulletproof as possible for any "enemy" to come forward and attack you.

❏ Have hair "did" and professionally styled so your look is sharp, sophisticated, and on point. Get nails done and a few on-point campaign outfits so you shine like a bright new penny. This is your big debut, so show the world you're a star!

❏ Oh, and please don't go robbing a bank or committing any crimes right before announcing to run!

CHAPTER 5

YOU CAN'T WIN ALONE:
CREATE YOUR ROCK STAR TEAM

"All of the real heroes are not storybook combat fighters either. Every single man in this Army plays a vital role. Don't ever let up. Don't ever think that your job is unimportant. Every man has a job to do and he must do it. Every man is a vital link in the great chain."
— **General George S. Patton, U.S. Army**

★ ★ ★

Y ou cannot win an election by yourself. I repeat, you cannot win an election by yourself. You may be the most awesome and qualified person, but it truly takes an army of supporters to make an impact with voters and win. It's essential that you create a support network that can rally around you, assisting you in operating your campaign. You need people you trust to advise you and give well-thought-out advice on strategies and tactics to win voters.

This group will be able to lend their wisdom as a sounding board, in addition to the campaign staff you will need to gather. You need people to boost your confidence, pick you up when you're feeling weak, and who can remind you to keep your eye on the prize and remain focused.

Get Family Support

Of course, the number one support that you can find is from your family. It's important that you discuss your desire and goals to run for office with your family for a number of reasons. First of all, their support — or lack thereof — will make a big influence on you throughout your campaign. It's also important — especially if you're married or have children — they will be directly impacted by your political career. Your family and partner will be put in the public eye, and scrutinized heavily. They also will have to deal with the fact that you will be very busy, and your campaign will have to take first priority for a large chunk of time. Even though you're the candidate, your family's actions, both current and past in many cases, will be in the spotlight, and up for election as well.

Once you have the support of family and friends, you're on your way to launching your campaign.

Next, you'll need to officially create your "rockstar campaign team."

Create your rockstar campaign team:

- **Campaign manager:** your campaign manager is your right-hand man (or woman) in helping to operate the campaign. Your campaign manager is knowledgeable about all aspects of campaigning and can deal with the day-to-day operations — you will be spending a ton of time with this person. It's important that this person is well-organized, resourceful, and has great communication skills.

- **Campaign consultant and strategist:** aside from a campaign manager, you may also have one or several consultants or strategists on your team who can help create your game plan and strategy to accomplish your goals and win your election. They also can offer good advice throughout your campaign.

- **Campaign treasurer:** definitely assign a treasurer if you are running for Congress, and for most other offices. Your treasurer should be a seasoned political campaign treasurer, since he or she needs to have a strong understanding of keeping all finances in check, reporting to the FEC (Federal Elections Committee), and be well versed with election financial rules and regulations. Obviously choose someone extremely honest, organized, and with a high level of integrity.

- **Public relations and media consultant:** a public relations (PR) consultant can help professionally present you and your campaign to news media outlets. A PR consultant should also be helpful with booking interviews and speaking opportunities. Other responsibilities include writing campaign literature, drafting speeches, and coordinating social media efforts. You may also consider having a separate social media manager, who focuses solely on managing and optimizing your social media game, but either way, you should have someone social media savvy who can help you leverage digital marketing.

- **Volunteer coordinator:** designate one person to coordinate volunteer efforts for your campaign. This is an integral part of seeing success among your supporters and potential voters. The volunteer coordinator will manage all efforts of the volunteers helping you spread your message to the community. Just a few things they will be tasked with organizing include managing volunteer events, setting up training, canvassing, and coordinating phone banks/campaigns.

Along with those essential campaign team positions, I recommend you also add these elements to your overall Rockstar team:

- **Create a prayer team.** Never, ever underestimate the power of prayer and prayer warriors! Prayers are powerful and effective for campaigns or any cause. A few months into my campaign, I started a *National Prayer Call*, every week and promoted it all over social media. I invited everyone to join the calls every week and pray for my campaign, our president, and our country. I led the prayer and invited other powerful pastors and evangelists on the call to lead prayers as well, including my friends Pastor Greg Young, Pastor Jack Hibbs, and Daniel Gelyana. It was very uplifting to have these calls every week and have "prayer warriors" from all over the nation unite over prayer. I recommend you do this too!

- **Create an Army of "Digital Soldiers."** Create an army of digital soldiers on social media. First, create "group chats" for your campaign within Twitter, Facebook, and Telegram to build your base of digital soldiers.

  I invited people I encountered through Twitter, Facebook, Instagram, and other places into these groups from all across the nation who showed enthusiasm and loyalty toward me and who wanted to help. They were the first to know about important updates in my campaign, posts, and tweets I wanted to spread, as well as things happening behind the scenes that I needed help protecting and defending against. They fended off attacks, shut down critics, and defended me with facts and evidence I provided them.

Honestly, these digital soldiers were the unsung heroes of my campaign and fought very hard for me behind the scenes. I could not have kept my campaign going and kept up my strength and positivity without them! I've never even met most of these great individuals in person, but they have become faithful friends. So, create these inner circle groups of digital soldiers for your campaign early on. Believe me, you'll need these online warriors later at some point.

- **Gather your "evangelists."** An evangelist in the sense I'm using it here is any person who spreads the good word about you to others. Your evangelists respect you, relate to your message, and essentially sell people on you, because they talk highly of you and vouch for you. They are important in building your reputation and helping to achieve a successful campaign, so you want to create as many evangelists as possible. That means meeting a lot of people, having conversations with them, and creating a lot of alliances. Meet prominent people in your district, get them to know you and like you so they spread the good word about you to others. Get to know members of your local GOP, city council, business organizations, churches, community centers, Rotary clubs, Knights of Columbus, and any other local groups in your area. Also, establish a relationship with other candidates running for office in other districts and even other states, so you can support one another and they can vouch for you, as well as defend you against any naysayers. This will help with the spread of positive information about you within their communities and groups, so you begin to have strong social proof and a positive reputation in your community, which is super important. Your reputation, your image, along with trust and respect of others, are key pieces in your ability to influence voters, gain national respect, and ultimately, win your election. You will not win in a vacuum being a social hermit.

On the campaign trail talking to the people!

I believe that If I had a national *popular vote*, I would have won in a landslide. I had so much support all across the nation and had so many alliances, friendships, and evangelists spreading the good word about me. However, because I was new to the district of San Francisco, I had the disadvantage of not knowing enough people in the district and no matter how fast I tried to establish relationships, my opponent had me beat on that front since he has lived in the area for 30 years and ran for office already four times, three of which were for this same position. If you are running in a district that is new to you, get started on developing key relationships early on, as far ahead as possible, and ideally long before you even announce that you're running for office. Become connected with the local GOP and key players I mentioned earlier, so you can start establishing a positive reputation and get people on your side before you officially start running.

Surround yourself ONLY with people you can trust. You've got to understand that when you are running for office, especially against well-known and deeply entrenched Swamp creatures like Nancy Pelosi, you will have an endless buffet of people approaching you, wanting to talk to you, and work with you. You will be spending a lot of time in social environments and hanging out with many new faces. Some of these people are trustworthy, however, many will appear to be benign, yet later will gossip about you or stab you in the back. You will hear more about malicious attacks in the next few chapters and this is why it is so important to be very careful who you trust.

It is essential that all those working on your campaign, even for one day, sign a non-disclosure agreement (NDA). Do not disclose any specific information, strategies, or ongoings about your campaign to anyone outside of your campaign team, unless you have them sign an NDA. Do not talk about anything personal or activities to anyone, even people you perceive as friends, unless you're okay with the information being spread. It may seem overly cautious, but it's better to be overprotective than not and have people leak things about you or your campaign that may end up damaging your campaign and reputation.

Line Up Endorsements, Alliances, Groups, asnd Organizations

Endorsements are an important aspect to giving your campaign more value and credibility if you secure several well-respected endorsements. Try to line these up even before you announce or in the earlier stages, with certain people you may already have in mind or find someone who can make those connections happen for you. Of course as you gain momentum and media attention, you'll have an easier time asking for and landing endorsements.

Action Items for securing endorsements:

- ❏ Create a list of those you admire and respect.

- ❏ Determine who would align well with your platform, policy, and positions, then list them as well.

- ❏ Think about which organizations would align well with your platform, policy, and positions and create a list.

- ❏ Make a short list of the great reasons why this person or organization should endorse you, but stay in the frame of mind that you're a badass and a rising star, so of course they should endorse you! They'd be silly not to. Start the conversation with confidence, assuming they'll say yes.

❏ Begin reaching out to every person and organization on all your lists. If you're having trouble reaching them directly, try to find other people or mutual connections you may have that can help you get in touch with them. Connect with them, have a conversation, and make *the* ask? The answer will always be no if you don't ask the question.

CHAPTER 6

CHOOSE YOUR FRIENDS (AND DATES) WISELY

"Don't be pushed around by the fears in your mind. Be led by the

dreams in your heart."

— Roy T. Bennett

I f you happen to be single, be very careful who you date. Be careful with whom you surround yourself and "who you hitch your wagon to," as they say in the political world. I unfortunately had to learn this lesson the hard way.

I will share with you a very uncomfortable situation that I wouldn't normally share, but it received some media coverage at the time, sadly. I figure you might as well hear it "from the horse's mouth" since there already have been some stories about it and it definitely did affect my campaign. I had the unfortunate experience of dating someone who started off well, but ended up turning into a horror story ripe for the "Inside Edition" series. Out of respect to him and the sensitive situation, I'm not going to use his real name and I'll refer to him as "Marco" from here on out.

If you're a single woman, or single man for that matter, and the goal for most is to eventually be married with a family, well then, the only way you're going to achieve that goal is by — duh — dating. Afterall, we must date in order to find Mr. or Mrs. Right, correct?

The problem is that our current culture, especially my millennial generation, is so messed up that there is a scarcity of quality people out there and we often end up spending time dating the wrong people. It's just the way it is. So, there I was at the start of 2019. I was pretty new to the political scene still, was meeting a lot of people, and attending many different events. During this time, I met someone and we became acquaintances. We ended up both speaking at political events, hanging out, and becoming even better friends.

We lived in the same city, too, so eventually, we tried the dating thing. This guy also happened to be a politician running for Congress, against a very high-profile figure. At the time I admired his boldness for taking on such a giant task, and we obviously shared a lot of the same interests and passions. I thought he was smart, brave, sweet, and passionate. We had some similar childhood experiences as well, so we connected.

He wasn't necessarily my typical "type," but I figured it would be a good thing to give someone different a chance who seemed like a nice guy and who wanted the same things in life as me. These days for many, it is very hard to find someone who shares your interests and values and who actually wants marriage and a family. It's almost become a rarity, sadly.

The relationship started off great and with potential. But a few months into it after spending more time together, I realized we were just not ultimately compatible. I tried to go back to being friends, because it seemed like we were better fitted for that. Well, lets just say he did not take this well. After I started breaking things off, a series of terrible events happened that I could never have imagined.

Marco started getting very aggressive, obsessive, and made it very clear to me: either I had to be with him completely, or he would "destroy" me and my life. I am someone who really can't help but be honest, so if I'm going to give my heart to someone and commit, I want to fully be in it and I just couldn't give him that.

So, destroy me he did. He took to the media and his social media accounts, which have more than half a million followers combined, to air out all his anger, and posted the most horrific lies and comments about me. I was dying of humiliation because I've always been of the mind that private relationship matters should stay private and be handled privately, not aired out for the world to see, on top of vicious slandering of someone you care about. He started keeping track of all my whereabouts and stalking me everywhere, while continuing to pressure and threaten me into staying with him. His behavior got progressively more obsessive and unstable. It escalated to the point where I finally had to take action to protect myself and file for a restraining order. In August of 2019, a Los Angeles Judge analyzed all the evidence and threats at our hearing and decided to grant me a five-year restraining order. I've never dealt with this kind of situation before but I thought after the order was granted, certainly he would back off now, because any rational person would stop harassing someone when they get a restraining order, right? Unfortunately, I thought dead *wrong*.

He got exponentially worse over the next six months, which I'll address later in the book.

CHAPTER 7

NO NUDES!

*"Whenever you see a successful person you only see the public
glories, never the private sacrifices to reach them."*
— Vaibhav Shah

★ ★ ★

Sharing is Not *Always* Caring

Remember in Chapter 4 when I talk about past choices coming back to haunt you? Well, I will once again swallow my pride and hope others will learn from past regrets of mine. So, I made the mistake of sending a few 'tasteful' nude photos to Marco early on in our relationship. At the time, we often think it's not going to be an issue because you trust this person and they would never violate that trust... right? *Ding Ding Ding!* That's the sound of the naive-o-meter breaking off. These kinds of things can always come back to haunt you. Sadly, it wasn't just the few 'tasteful' nude photos that haunted me.

Imagine someone hacking into your email accounts and having access to every email you've sent or received from more than 10 years ago? Imagine someone hacking into your iCloud account and having access to every video or picture you've saved from early adulthood? Imagine someone telling you that they hired private investigators to follow you around everywhere for the last year, document you, and dig up all of your records? Imagine an ex-boyfriend telling you he secretly videotaped you when you were together in moments you thought were private. Imagine someone telling you they were spying on you *through the camera* on your laptop and cell phone for months, when you had no idea.

Imagine if you owned a business and someone hacked into your company files, pulled all your client and customer information, threatened to kill your business and cut off your only source of income? Imagine waking up in the mornings and seeing terrible, embarrassing tweets and pictures posted from YOUR OWN Twitter account, because your Twitter was hacked overnight while you slept. Imagine someone blowing up your phone from countless different "aliases" and phone numbers at all times, and tracking all of your whereabouts, so that you could never really get any peace.

I don't have to imagine this, because this IS what happened to me. This is what I was dealing with for months behind the scenes while at the same time trying to run my campaign against the most vicious high-profile congresswoman today.

These weren't just empty threats either that I could brush off, they were real and terrifying. The individual doing this isn't just a normal average Joe. He is a relatively high-profile person with a huge following and well connected to influential people in political circles, as well as the media. So, his threats weren't just things I could roll off my back, they carried serious repercussions to my career, my future, and my safety.

Marco actually sent me pictures of myself while I was out and about, or while socializing with friends just to send me warnings that he "was always following me." He sent me pictures of myself through the camera on my computer; which is a level of feeling violated that is just hard to describe. When he told me he was doing that I actually had to research it, because I didn't even know it was possible to do that — and yes, it's very possible to do this and apparently perverted men do this all the time to unsuspecting women! I eventually got in a habit of covering my cameras with duct tape and I encourage you to cover your cameras as well.

He used the information he illegally obtained to blackmail and extort me for months. As much as I tried to reason with him and get him to stop, he persisted, and I unfortunately became a virtual hostage to this gangstalking.

He would call and text relentlessly with threats like, "I'm going to destroy your career and life unless you get back together with me," or I'm going to have XYZ published in the media tomorrow, if you don't see me or call me today." Or, "I'm going to get you cancelled from speaking at XYZ event that I see you're scheduled to speak at, unless you see me." Then he would start a creepy "countdown" process. Since I refused to see him or give in to any of his other demands, I figured I would settle for a call to him here and there or respond to him to keep him from fully pulling the trigger on the virtual gun he was holding to my head to extort me.

There also was the fear of the unknown that kept me complying. What did he have that was so bad? What was this "career-ending" or "life-ending" video or piece of information that he had on me? Even though I could not think of anything I did in the past that would be that bad, the fear of the unknown held me hostage.

Interestingly enough, there is an Alinsky tactic within *Rules for Radicals* that states, "The threat is usually more terrifying than the thing itself." It's a psychological manipulation tactic that is widely used by both politicians and criminals, and I understand why — it works.

I'm so ashamed that this happened, because I consider myself such a smart and strong woman and usually don't take crap from anyone. Especially someone trying to pressure me! Yet somehow I fell into this trap and allowed myself to be in such a position.

I share this with you, because I want to be transparent about my journey, but I also want you to learn from my lessons. Don't put yourself in a position where you ever could be a hostage to blackmail and extortion like I was.

If you've ever sent 'intimate' photos to anyone, try to track those people down and ask them to either delete them or sign NDAs. Remove any compromising photos from any dating sites as well. Your friends or exes may not comply, but at least you can try. Change all your passwords to all of your social media, phone, email accounts, anything online for that matter, change them regularly, and make them super strong. I am one of those people who used simple passwords previously and thought it was silly to have passwords that had a zillion different characters in them, because how the heck do you remember them? Behold the wisdom of the engineers and tech nerds.

Cover your camera on your laptop with duct tape when it's not in use. Start living your life as if your opposition's private investigators are watching always. They may not be, but if your opponent really wants dirt on you, they will find a way to get it at all costs.

Trust very few people, and don't be too open. The circle of people and friends who I have come to *really* trust has shrunk dramatically since I've been in the political world. Unfortunately, I learned the hard way that politics is a very dirty game and people who were once your friend or pretend to be your friend can turn on a dime and backstab you. Also, money makes some people do dirty things.

Be careful when you're out at public events or socializing. Keep it classy, don't drink much in public nor at political events, and don't get sloppy — there is someone always watching and waiting to spill the tea.

Sadly, slut-shaming is also very real in politics. *'But, I'm not a slut, so how can they slut-shame me?!'* I thought. Oh dear friend, they'll find a way. If you are a single man in the political world, you will probably be smeared as a "womanizer." If you are a single woman, you will probably be smeared as a slut. That's why so many people get married and stay married in politics — for the optics of it. It's good optics to have a partner by your side and that's especially true in the Republican world. I'm just being real. These are the things no one tells you, so don't find out the hard way. Women can be extremely jealous and catty. They are often the ones subtly pulling other women down and they're the biggest rumor spreaders. Don't underestimate the two-faced gossip capabilities of the sweet old ladies who appear innocent!

You also may want to ask *yourself* an honest question: do you find yourself being that woman who feels a bit jealous of other women who are in the spotlight, and try to subtly tear them down and attack their character behind their backs? Be honest. If this is you, then let's be real, you are part of this problem, too. We've all been there sometimes and felt that way when others are gaining success, I get it. But I've seen a lot of in-fighting among women since getting deeper in politics, and patriot women will tear down the entire movement if we focus on tearing down each other instead of tearing down our real enemy and taking back our country.

★ ★ ★

Be Careful Who You're Seen With — Eyes are Always on You!

If you're a woman, spend more time with female rather than male colleagues in public. I had to learn the hard way that it is simply the nature of the beast that women will spread rumors about other women and will slut-shame for absolutely no reason other than your shirt may not be high enough or you're hanging out with a male colleague at an event.

At the start of my campaign, I attended that California Republican Convention (CRC) for the weekend in Indio, California. It was my first ever CRC so I was excited, but also a little nervous. I bought some classy and beautiful new outfits, got my hair done and wanted to make it a productive weekend that would give my budding campaign a boost. The friend that I was talking about earlier, "Rob," told me he'd help me out by introducing me to people and helping me feel comfortable there since he served in many high positions in the CA GOP and knew everyone. He introduced me to some great people and we hung out a lot throughout the conference, which I didn't think was a big deal because I spent time talking to many other people at the conference, too and I have a lot of friends, both male and female. What could possibly go wrong? Ooh boy.

The Monday after the conference, a certain blogger who runs a certain website and newsletter with a large Republican following, wrote a recap of the convention. He started a rumor that I was this individual's *"young new girlfriend"* and the rumor spread that he was my *"Sugar Daddy."* I was infuriated. I wanted to scream! All that hard work meeting great people and establishing new relationships just to be negated by something so stupid and false. I had already just dealt with all the fake news and BS with the ex-boyfriend situation, so the last thing I wanted was more misinformation circulating at the start of my campaign. It didn't matter how many times I corrected people and told people that we were strictly platonic friends and I was not, in fact, sleeping with nor dating this man; people are straight savages and they just love to tear down an up-and-coming young woman who's making waves.

Also, keep your friends from posting pictures of you on their social media profiles, too. My RINO opponent saw a picture of me on a friend's Instagram with a male friend's arm around me, and another male friend's arm around her, as well as an Instagram story of us out joking around and singing to music. Can't I still have some fun sometimes during a break from campaigning? The next morning I woke up and there's an article written up about me with the headline *"DeAnna talks about God, family, and country by day and parties like a rock star at night!"* Ughhh. REALLY?!

As a millennial Italian who is a warm and outgoing person and used to sharing casual pictures of friends on social media, this took some getting used to. I'm also naturally more of a tomboy at heart, since I was raised with four brothers so I have a lot of male friends and am just comfortable around them.

Growing up with four rowdy brothers and a bunch of male cousins and uncles — and all of their friends — I often even found being around male friends is easier than being around only women. Not because I want to date them or "sleep with" them for God's sake. However, women can carry a lot of unnecessary drama and a lot of gossip and sensitivity, while males are typically just easy-going and funny. It was just part of my upbringing and I never thought of this as a big deal. *Whoops!* If you are a younger, bold, relatively attractive person, then others, especially women, may be threatened by you, hate on you, and look for any reason whatsoever to try to make you look bad. And if they can't find anything, they will often make up utter lies about you out of their behinds. It's absolutely disgusting that they act like this and it was a rude awakening for me that I'm frankly still getting used to since I've always just been a straight shooter. If I have a question about someone or an issue with them, I will talk to them to their face about it and move on. I don't do the whole "gossip behind their back" thing, but I've found that most people do in this world, and it just is what it is. You may not be able to avoid all of the hating, but you can at least take measures to bullet-proof yourself as much as possible to smears, gossip, and misinformation.

Action Items:

❏ Have fun and get to know new people, but be very cautious in sharing too much.

❏ Before getting serious with someone, consider conducting background checks and/or looking through their social media accounts to try to get a better sense for who they are for peace of mind.

❏ Watch how they treat other people, and try to find friends or former friends who know this person and ask about them.

❏ Take the relationship very slowly at first and don't reveal too much or "hitch your wagon" to someone until you're absolutely sure.

CHAPTER 8

DOCUMENT YOUR JOURNEY

"Incredible change happens in your life when you decide to take control of what you do have power over, instead of craving control over what you don't."
— **Steve Maraboli**

O ne of the most important lessons in public relations, and life for that matter, is to get your message out first so you have *control* of the message you want to communicate. One of the best ways to share your message and your story is by documenting it through photography and videography. Afterall, a picture is worth a thousand words, right? Whether you run for public office, you're championing a cause, or you're wanting to elevate your platform and be known as a political rockstar, hire a photographer and or videographer to document your journey. Make them a part of your journey. If budget is an issue, which it was for me at the start of my campaign, you most likely can find an eager intern or recent college grad to work with you very inexpensively.

As much as I can't stand AOC, I must admit she did a phenomenal job of mastering her online and social media game. She built an enormous following and people fell in love with her, because they felt like they were part of her journey. She posted pictures and videos along her campaign trail that told a story of an ordinary girl who appeared sensitive, compassionate, brave, and relatable. Who knows how many of her pictures and videos were "staged," but they accomplished her mission at the end of the day by capturing hearts and minds. And of course, that led to her ultimate victory over her deeply entrenched Democratic incumbent. Elizabeth Warren attempts the same thing sometimes with her lame "hold my beer" videos, but at least she has the right idea. Remember, we're entering a "new school" of politics where people don't just want to elect a polished politician — they want to elect a real person who they feel like they know.

I did the same thing with my own journey. As soon as I decided I was going to run for office, I began my search for a photographer/videographer to follow me along on my campaign trail. I wanted to document my campaign — the good, the bad, and the ugly of it. I wanted people to know what went on behind the scenes and really get to know me. I also wanted to document everything so that I could counter any possible "fake news" that might be published along the way and show the real story of what happened during those moments. My photographer also became a great friend and confidante during the rollercoaster of the journey. He saw me at my best and at my worst, but always helped me capture the beautiful moments that brought my vision to life. There were only a few events where I did not bring him along because I "didn't think it was needed," but we regretted it after!

Some of the highlights of my campaign immortalized on film and photography include:

- Capturing the smiles and expressions of gratitude on the faces of the homeless Americans when giving food and listening to them.

- Capturing the roaring cheers, the standing ovations, and expressions of the hundreds of people who jumped for joy and cried once they heard I was running against Nancy Pelosi.

- Capturing the faces of men and women who looked at me with such hope in their eyes, that something could possibly change for the better.

- Capturing the moments when I broke down and cried, because I felt weak, discouraged, and exhausted.

- Capturing the moments of sheer pride when we accomplished an incredible feat in the campaign.

- Capturing conversations with the American people of all races and walks of life who touched my heart or opened my mind.

Your campaign isn't just a campaign; it's a story to be told. Share that story. Share *your* story.

There are so many amazing photos and videos that my photographer and I captured along the campaign trail, but I'm limited to how many I can publish here. If you'd like to see many more moments and footage, visit my website at www.DeannaLorraine.com and my YouTube channel at YouTube.com/c/DeAnnaLorraine

Talking to the sailors and veterans during Fleet Week.

Action Items:

- ❏ Consider hiring a photographer and videographer for your campaign.

- ❏ Create your first campaign video ad.

- ❏ Take campaign headshots.

- ❏ Start journaling your experience to potentially share with others later.

**Make sure that you're a part of my growing community of fearless patriots as we fight together in the war of our lives to take back America. Join my Inner Circle email list and Telegram group —this is our "safe space" to freely communicate about all of these issues, organize, mobile rallies and other important actions that we need to take to fight back & take back America:
DeannaLorraine.com/inner-circle.

*Also be sure you subscribe to my Podcast, **Taking Back America!** I broadcast every Tuesday, Wednesday & Thursday from **YouTube, Periscope, iTunes,** and other channels and I keep you updated on the latest breaking news as well as my upcoming events.*

YouTube.com/c/DeAnnaLorraine

Twitter.com/DeAnna4Congress

CHAPTER 9

BE YOUR OPPONENT'S NUMBER ONE TROLL

"The art of war teaches us to rely not on the likelihood of the enemy's not coming, but on our own readiness to receive him; not on the chance of his not attacking, but rather on the fact that we have made our position unassailable."
— **Sun Tzu**

If you're running for public office, it is imperative that you become an expert on your opponent — and learn all their juicy dirt, sins, and weaknesses! Nancy Pelosi was my main opponent obviously, so I learned everything about her. I got news alerts on her, and was watching her like a hawk every day, putting constant pressure on her and attacking her. I also was constantly drawing stark contrasts between her and me.

I was notified as soon as she tweeted and would try to be the first one to leave a sassy comment in the thread — I must say, she made it pretty fun and easy to draw contrasts. For starters, she barely speaks coherently and sounds drunk most of the time. I thoroughly enjoyed making video montages of back-to-back soundbites of her

101

sounding like a drunk, with me sounding sharp and sober. And hey, should the position even be called "Speaker of the House" if the individual in the position can't even speak coherently??

A few things I discovered about my "nasty" nemesis include:

- She blatantly prioritized the sham impeachment of Trump and spent all her days obsessing about how "horrible" he is, meanwhile her own district of San Francisco was rotting with homelessness, trash, drugs, feces, and crime. This made it easy for me to point out her sheer negligence of the issues that really matter to most Americans.

- When Nasty Nancy isn't spewing lies and vitriol at the president, she spends the other half of her time prioritizing the well-being of illegal immigrants. She talks endlessly about the "kids in cages," yet spends zero time talking about the Americans who have lost their lives, because they were killed by criminal illegals, or the thousands of lives lost to opioids, homelessness, or human trafficking.

- To illustrate these points further, my team and I went scouring through her official campaign website and we discovered that Nancy Pelosi's campaign had released more than 361 press releases in the past year — and *not a single one* addressed the homelessness crisis. All of her press releases focused on impeachment, immigration, and LGBTQ issues. This was a great find! We created a press release out of these findings and shared it all over the media. These became great talking points during my campaign, because I could correlate her negligence and backwards priorities with real data. When I shared this data with locals and homeless individuals in San Francisco, they actually were shocked and it made them open up and think. I may have even been able to change some minds due to it.

If you're running against a highly visible and famous person, like Nancy Pelosi, you might be worried about attacking them, because you're afraid of them attacking you back. I know I was a little worried about that, too, at first, especially knowing the massive number of their social media followings. Yikes. However, fear not — you WANT them to say your name!

If they say your name, that's free press and gives you more attention.

If they happen to mention your name or publicly call you out, stand by your statements and don't retract. Just make sure that what you say when you attack them is factually correct, so you won't need to backpedal later with your tail between your legs. In all likelihood though, the chances of your famous opponent actually talking about you in public is very low. They most likely will just ignore you, because they also know that mentioning your name would only give you more press. So, knowing this should give you free reign to attack away.

DeAnna Lorraine 🏳️ ✅
@DeAnna4Congress

I'm DeAnna Lorraine, Conservative Sicilian spitfire running against Nancy Pelosi for Congress. I will replace her soulless leadership with love, laws, & fierce patriotism.

Tick-tock Old Nan, your day of reckoning is coming for your crimes against Americans ⏰ 🔥
#ByeNancy

1:53 | 2.1M views

One of my most popular tweets that was retweeted by President Trump.

Continue to illustrate for your supporters and voters how your opponent is shady, selfish, out of touch with the problems of the district, or whatever the reasons are that he or she should be voted out and you should be elected. Since you will be listening to the concerns of your "people," you should be able to articulate those issues and concerns they have in public and be a voice for them. Using your platform as a voice for them will have them appreciating you. You wouldn't believe the number of grateful messages I receive from people all over the country for constantly calling out Nancy whenever she said something crazy, unfair, disrespectful, or dishonest.

I became Nasty Nancy's number one troll. I also had other Democrat opponents in my race, of course. I did not pay much attention to my three other Democratic opponents, because: a) they were surprisingly respectful, kept their focus on their own campaigns, and never attacked me; and, b) It would have been a waste of my time. It's usually a waste of your time to attack your other opponents in the race aside from your main opponent, if they are minding their own business, because it only draws more attention to them.

However, my RINO opponent was a different story. At first, I tried to just ignore him, stay focused on Nancy and "keep it classy." I figured he should just campaign and run his own race, I will focus on my own campaign, and let the voters decide to let the best man or woman win, right? That would have been sweet, but I soon had to become his number one troll, too.

After JD's insulting comments about me during the CA Republican Convention, I knew that where there was smoke — there was probably fire — and that fire started smoldering quickly. On the Sunday morning of that same convention, a group of colleagues and I were sitting down chatting in the hotel lobby — when we looked up and saw JD sneakily walk around the lobby corner with none other than my ex, Marco, who was also a delegate at the convention. Then they both hurriedly ran outside the hotel doors to secretly meet away from the hotel, as if they were two fugitives in the night. What could they possibly be meeting about?

Well, JD took advantage of the hostile situation with my vindictive ex and started working with him to get "dirt" on me that he would then use to slander me and try to sabotage my campaign. The two of them began a very mutually beneficial relationship, much like parasites with me as the host. Marco used JD as a proxy to retaliate against me and extort me into trying to get back together with him and/or drop the restraining order; JD used Marco to do his dirty work for him in gaining leverage and undermining my campaign. Marco raised more than a million dollars in his last campaign and had quite a war chest built up of donors, email lists, media contacts, and other resources. So, he would scratch JD's back by boosting his social media, sharing all his resources, and giving him "info" on me. A number of people talked to JD about the situation and told him he should back off from befriending or working with Marco. JD apparently did not care though and he happily kept working with him, because he was reaping the benefits of Marco's retaliation efforts against me. My ex would taunt me all the time by telling me he would give all of those things to *me* instead of JD, if only I would just "come to my senses" and get back together with him. But it was so wrong the way he was going about it that I couldn't do that. It just wasn't right to be with someone only out of pressure, fear, or in exchange for resources. Some women may say that's dumb; some marry men only for "resources" and then divorce a few years later, taking them to the cleaners. That may float some women's boats, but I've never been that kind of woman and I wasn't going to start now.

Any man who could work with someone who he *knows* is violating an active restraining order and continuously harassing and stalking the woman who obtained the order, has GOT to be dirty and unethical, I figured.

So, upon further investigation, I discovered that Mr. RINO's campaign manager, a slick, smarmy, silver-haired man by the name of Clint Griess, was no saint either. I'm going to just refer to this individual throughout the book as "Grease Ball," because I found out early on in my campaign that many locals refer to him as this nickname behind his back, and for good reason. In fact, after some digging around I discovered that he had been a longtime member of the "Peace and Freedom Party," which is a *radical Socialist party*, until very recently. He only just registered as a Republican for the first time when he became JD's campaign manager. He had even been a paid staffer and political operative for the current radical Democratic mayor of San Francisco, London Breed. To add to the shadiness, I found out Grease Ball had even previously tried to get the SF GOP to endorse Breed, even when two solid Republicans also were running in that race for Mayor and vying for the GOP endorsement. In the past year, he and JD had cozied up together and were virtually joined at the hip. He became JD's campaign manager, and then, JD also "installed" him as the new executive director of the SF GOP. Now why would someone who had been a Socialist for many years now be working for a Republican's campaign and be his BFF? And, why would he be fit to be the executive director of the SF GOP? It was odd and felt all kinds of shady, to say the least.

Here's an excerpt about Grease Ball from an article published by prominent political reporter, Steve Frank:

"You can't make this stuff up! Just how bad off is the Republican party in San Fran? The new executive director

was a member of the Peace and Freedom Party just a year ago. Then he became an NPP voter. On August 8 — less than a month ago he registered as a Republican."

"He worked for radical Democrat London Breed for Mayor of San Fran — and tried to get the San Fran GOP to endorse her, even though TWO GOP'ers were also running for Mayor."

"Clint then became the campaign manager for former Libertarian Caucus leader John Dennis in his race for District Supervisor last year."

"Now Griess is both the executive director of the San Fran GOP — with Chairman John Dennis, and the campaign manager for the John Dennis for Congress effort against San Fran Nan Pelosi. As executive director of the SF GOP, Griess is now eligible to receive confidential information from the CRP and other Republican organizations."[9]

There was also the entire "conflict of interest" issue that JD continued to deny. How can someone be both the *chairman* of the SF GOP, and also run for the *Congressional* seat in the same district at the same time, especially if another Republican also is running for that seat? Many concerned people talked to him about this conflict of interest and asked him to choose one position or the other, but that he needed to step down from one so the lines wouldn't get blurred. He kept denying that there is any conflict of interest and stubbornly refused to step down from either position, meanwhile the meetings and environment within the SF GOP sphere grew increasingly toxic due to his anger and jealousy of my blooming campaign. It was such a shame too, because there were actually some very nice, decent people in the SF GOP with whom I was trying to get to know and befriend. Not all the members of the GOP were bad or hostile to me, but JD and Grease Ball poisoned the well so much and made it so awkward with the group, putting so much pressure on members to not talk to me and getting furious if they found out about anyone befriending me. The unethical conflict of interest issue became blindingly apparent as the months wore on, especially when it came to the endorsements for our congressional race. But, we'll get to that later.

Just like I did with Nancy, I got to know JD's chinks in his armor and started using the same compare-and-contrast strategy I was deploying with her: he was old, I was youthful. He ran for 10 years and a proven loser, I am a fresh up-and-comer with loads of potential. He is a boring, low-energy, abysmal communicator and public speaker; I'm a high-energy, powerful, engaging speaker who draws enthusiasm and crowds. He appears contrived and rehearsed, I'm authentic and I tell it like it is.

He pretends like he's perfect and better than everyone; I am self-deprecating and embrace my imperfections. He speaks from a script; I speak from the heart. Over time, people saw these differences on their own and started coming around to me. I became known as "the people's candidate," while he became known as the Establishment "Mitt Romney" candidate who is out of touch with the people.

I also quickly realized that he is a bit of a control freak and hates to be caught off guard. So, what did I do? Showed up places where he wasn't expecting me and stole his thunder, of course! Over time, I grew so many enthusiastic supporters that they would be voluntarily doing the trolling for me. We discovered along the way that he has very thin skin and would get easily triggered and nasty to people who made comments on social media that he didn't like. So, when my followers called him out about something on his Twitter, he would, like clockwork, degrade and insult them. Then they would post screenshots of his nasty comments to them and to others. It was fun! This brought more and more supporters to my side, and turned many away from him as word spread like wildfire that he was an arrogant jerk.

As my campaign continued to pick up speed, I started getting flooded with "JD refugees" — people who started out following him, but then got turned off when his true colors showed — and fled over to the warm, positive atmosphere I generated. My space was the "safe space!" Ha-ha.

Our President Trump is the *master troll*. He knows just what to say to get under his enemy's skin and gets them to react in such a way that exposes their true colors. *If you want to win, be your opponent's number one troll.*

CHAPTER 10

KEEP IT REAL, BABY

"If you are going to do something truly innovative, you have to be someone who does not value social approval. You can't need social approval to go forward."
— **Malcolm Gladwell**

Speak Your Mind and Follow Your Instincts

Throughout my campaign, people tried to bend and mold me in all sorts of different directions. People tried to give me ALL sorts of different advice.

A smattering of some of the useless advice I was given included:

- Change my campaign slogan, and take "God" out of it — because "San Francisco is too secular and God isn't really a thing here."

- Hide my support for Trump. Because moderates may be offended.

- Don't talk about legal immigration, borders, or building the Wall, because San Francisco is a Sanctuary City with a lot of illegal immigrants and they may be offended.

- Talk more "politically correct" and sensitive.

- Run as an Independent instead of a Republican.

- Don't talk about the family unit and traditional values, because of the huge LGBTQ community in the district, who may be offended.

- Don't say I'm pro-life, because all the pro-choice liberals in the district would hate me for it.

Welp, I stuck to my guns and kept my slogan "God, Family, Country." I liked it, it felt right, and it summed up what my mission was, both for the campaign and beyond, as what I believed to be the antidote for healing America.

I continued to be a proud and loud supporter of our President Trump. I may not always talk about him in every single interaction and setting, but I sure as hell wasn't going to neuter all my social media posts and speeches just to try to pander and appeal more to the left and center.

Instead of acting evasive over the abortion issue, I went to a massive pro-life rally right in San Francisco and had my own booth set up all day with volunteers. I even grabbed a megaphone and marched through the streets yelling about the need to restore God, family, and morality back into our country and become a nation that celebrates life once again, rather than death and abortion on demand. Although perhaps I could have gained more votes by running as an Independent, I did not want to run as an independent, because I felt like that would just be dishonest. I have strong views and strong values, so pretending like I was in the "middle of the road" or lukewarm on so many issues about which I was passionate just to get more votes did not feel right to me. Plus, the honest truth is that I had a high chance of losing my Primary race, due to all of the challenges of the California election system and the data of my race in particular. And if I was going to lose, I wanted to "lose" with a bang. I wanted to be remembered for the causes that I championed and my strong stances on Conservative issues; not someone who bent myself into a pretzel so much to appease other people that I was just a shell of my real self afterwards. Weak people will stand for nothing and fall for everything. I wanted to be someone who stood my ground and not wavered just out of pressure. What kind of representative would I be then, if elected? A sell-out, that's who I'd be and that's definitely not who I am.

We CANNOT have any more weak and spineless politicians. That's one of the main reasons why we're in this mess to begin with!

And that's my other rule: *Trust and follow your instincts.*

If you want to be a true, fearless firebrand who is successful in politics and makes a tangible impact in this world, you need to get in the habit of relying on your instincts more and trusting them. So many people will try to give you advice and it can get very confusing with so much different information, different options to take, and different choices to make when leading. That's why it's essential that you start sharpening your intuition and learning how to recognize it more clearly, when you're running for office or before so you can be prepared when life gets even more noisy.

I learned how to trust and follow my instincts throughout my campaign and they have continued to serve me well, almost all the time. My instinct was telling me that as much as people tried to "tame" me or be a certain way, or shut my mouth on certain issues, I needed to just keep it real and stay honest and true to who I am all the way through. Even if it costs me votes.

My opponent JD ran three times already against Nancy, and a fourth time for the district supervisor race. He was soft and vague about where he stood on issues, and even admitted he was intentional about appearing non-committal since he was trying to appeal to all and avoid offending anyone. According to an article from *The New York Times* in 2010: "Mr. Dennis is not exactly leading with his party affiliation." Dennis said, "I don't usually include the Republican *part*."[10] Good grief, way to stand up for your values.

I never once heard him talking about faith nor God. I never heard him make comments openly supporting President Trump. Well, he started finally saying that he supported Trump months into his campaign when he saw that I was doing so and he realized that it was "cool" to talk about Trump with the MAGA crowd. I never heard him voice strong stances on any issues for that matter, like immigration, free speech, our Second Amendment, or the struggles of our current culture and spiritual war. His method seemed to be "remain neutral and vanilla," to appeal to more voters and decrease the odds of offending people.

But, how did that work for him? Well, he lost miserably in each of his four previous races. My personal belief is that when you try to appear too neutral and soft so you can appeal to everyone, you end up appealing to no one, because no one understands your views strongly enough to resonate with them. So, I figured I would listen to my gut and keep being myself, stay real, and people are either going to gravitate toward me and love me for it, or they'll be repelled by it, but I was willing to take that chance and at least make a big splash. Vanilla was never my ice cream flavor anyway.

One thing about me is, I can't be put in a box or corralled into a cage. Try to label me all you want, but you'll fail epically since I simply cannot be labeled. I'm multi-dimensional. I'm bold. I like to do crazy things that shake people up and get an important message across. I'm also very compassionate and have a huge heart for people who I feel are being ignored or treated unfairly, and I've always been compelled to stand up for them. I'm honest, possibly to a fault. I seek the truth and speak the truth, even when it might not be popular or politically correct. And if you really want to know if your a$$ looks fat in those jeans, then don't ask me, because I don't do the fake stuff well and I'll actually give you the true answer.

Yeah, I love God and my faith in Him is strong. I believe if more Americans developed their faith and we got back to being a country that put Judeo-Christian values in our culture, we'd be a much stronger and greater nation. I'm also not a "saint." I go out with my friends, drink sometimes, have a good time, and let my hair down. So what? I'm a passionate woman, but I absolutely despise the sexual hook-up culture. And, don't you dare tell me that I don't have faith in God or I'm a bad Christian, because I'm not perfect. I might not be perfect, but I may be the perfect messenger for the current time. I personally find it hard to relate to someone who seems perfect in every way and leads a picture-perfect life, because it seems like they are "up there" talking down at me. I feel the best messengers and leaders are those to whom we can relate, who can share and teach from a real place, from their own personal experiences and challenges. Perfect is so yesterday. *Realness* is what's hot today.

Our great Trump is the same way — he keeps it real. His authenticity and defiance of traditional political norms are what make him such a breath of fresh air, winning over the hearts of so many people far and wide who were disgusted with the same old, used-car-salesmen-style of puppet politicians. He also has great instincts, and follows them — which often leads him to victories.

I call Trump the "Happy Gilmore of the political world." Before he came along, the political world was stuffy, old, arrogant, and boring.

The RINOs are like the "Shooter McGavins," snobby and elitist, expecting to win on their clout and facade of perfection. Then, Happy Gilmore came along like a bat out of hell and disrupted the whole golf game, making it fun, interesting, and exciting to watch. He brought in a whole new colorful crowd of many different types of people who weren't necessarily interested in golf before, but came to see him. Think about it — Trump's rallies are totally like Happy Gilmore's golf tournaments — colorful, rowdy, fun, and welcoming to everyone. The "Establishment" professional golfers couldn't stand it, but got left in the dust in the end.

Some of the actual leaders of the California GOP have said publicly that "Republicans must look and sound more like California Democrats to be viable in our state, to essentially be Republican-lite." They even have said that Republicans should avoid openly talking about their support for the president, if they do support him, along with the core issues he champions, because that could potentially "turn off" people. Gee, and you wonder why the California GOP has been failing over the years and California has become more and more blue!

My friend Christy Marie McLaughlin is another young Republican woman, currently running for Congress in Florida's 19th congressional district. She had this to say about keeping it real and standing up for your beliefs:

"To run for office is a service to the community. The moment I announced my candidacy, people from every corner of our country approached me and tried to direct me on how to run my candidacy and what issues I should focus on. As an advocate for Conservative beliefs, I have faced many forms of antagonism and impediments, ranging from a pat on the head to "stay in your lane, little girl" to more contentious and severe attacks, but they do not phase me. Running for office is my chariot to use my voice to protect and defend personal liberties."

"When I was in law school, my constitutional law professor, at my very left-wing school, sauntered in wearing a "Make America Great Again" hat. The classroom immediately burst into chuckles, and I didn't quite understand the joke. But then, my professor greeted the class with a fake nasally Southern accent. He proceeded to perform an entire skit playing a

mentally challenged Trump supporter whose other idols included Napoleon Bonaparte and Forrest Gump. That moment crystalized my determination to no longer be silenced and actively speak up about my Conservative beliefs, because if my professors could use their classrooms as propaganda tools, then I had a right to fight it. If I didn't share my voice, then I was doing a disservice to myself and other students. Experiences like these prepared me for my run for public office and thickened my skin, because I've experienced so much more hostility now that I'm more visible. A candidate should always have their ears open to other perspectives, but should firmly stand by their beliefs and not falter to influence. I refuse to allow hostility to scare me from openly advocating for President Trump and the Republican Party."

Be authentic. Be approachable and even *vulnerable* sometimes. Whoever you are, just embrace it. You may be more of the strict Conservative type, you may be more of the anti-Establishment Happy Gilmore/Trump type. Or, you may not fit in any box. Be you, stand up for your values and make a hot brand out of *you*, instead of trying to bend yourself into a pretzel to try to fit in. People will respect that more than a sell-out. If your heart is in the right place and your intentions are pure, then you are good enough and perfect exactly how you are.

Remember, too, that right now we are at war — and we need ordinary Americans to do badass extraordinary things to reclaim America. In order to make real progress in returning our country to greatness, we're going to have to take the gloves off and get past all the "trigger words" and safe spaces. My generation doesn't have time to worry about trigger words, because we have some really important work to do together. And some really important public, honest conversations to have that are going to require us breaking the shackles of political correctness to be messengers for *truth*, and wake people up! If you're not a "perfect" person, think about how you can instead convey yourself as the perfect *messenger for the job*, for the current time.

CHAPTER 11

GET DIRTY,
DANCE IN THE RAIN

"Inaction breeds doubt and fear. Action breeds confidence and courage. If you want to conquer fear, do not sit home and think about it. Go out and get busy."
— **Dale Carnegie**

If you want to be a true fearless leader who makes a real impact, then take your damn Prada high heels off, roll up your sleeves, and get to work! There are so many leaders, influencers, and politicians in this world who don't actually do any "dirty work." They do nothing, but talk and thumb their noses at people, while they stay comfy and clean in their gated mansions or high-rise apartments.

Set yourself apart as a leader by demonstrating that you have a solid work ethic and you are a "doer," not just a "talker." Show the world your grit and determination, rain or shine, whether it's comfortable or not to do so.

Early in my campaign when I first started planting roots in San Francisco, I took on the attitude that I would be the *Rosie the Riveter* candidate, willing to roll up my sleeves and face problems head-on. This is especially important if you're a pretty girl or a preppy-looking "pretty boy." Unfortunately, people often will have a preconceived notion of you that you aren't the type of person who can get dirty and do real work. Prove them wrong — and have fun doing it.

You also can bet that many of the "older" Establishment politicians will not do work or get "dirty." They think they're too good for that and they assume they can skate by with just their name or clout without having to disrupt their precious comfort level.

I decided to kick off my entrance into the city with a bang and set the record straight about who I was as a person. You may recall our great President Trump created a huge media frenzy and put San Francisco in the spotlight when he started making comments about the horrific conditions of the city, saying, "They have to clean it up. We can't have our cities going to hell." This brought attention to the fact that complaints of human waste on public streets and sidewalks in San Francisco skyrocketed by 400 percent in the last decade — all on Nancy Pelosi's watch. Lots of people were talking about it. I decided we had to take action. Enough talk and political grandstanding!

I was fresh off the big cleanup with the famous Conservative activist Scott Presler in Los Angeles and witnessed what a productive and positive experience it was for all involved. I joined him along with dozens of other volunteers as we cleaned up a homeless encampment and shoveled up more than 50 tons of trash. It was dirty and gross, but so rewarding and lots of fun.

I asked Scott to organize a cleanup with me in San Francisco, because it needed it so badly, and he said he definitely would, but wouldn't be able to until at least February due to his schedule being so full for months. I could have waited until February, but that was over four months away and honestly, it didn't seem right to wait that long. If the city needed attention, it needed attention *immediately,* and it seemed inauthentic to wait four months to clean up the streets just so that I could utilize the extra clout and media attention that Scott would probably bring. I asked him if he would be okay if I organized my own cleanup in San Francisco in the near future and he would partner with me on the next one later on when he was available. With his blessing, I initiated this cleanup, planned, and promoted it. I couldn't even imagine Nancy Pelosi or my other opponents wearing a hazmat suit and picking up trash in the dirty streets for hours, but their lack of interest in "getting dirty" became my opportunity and advantage. No one had ever led a "cleanup effort" in San Francisco before, shockingly, but I wanted to do something really positive for the city right from the onset and show people that although I was the new kid on the block, I was there to work, contribute, and serve.

My team and I sent out a press release to the media with all the details and planned everything in just two weeks. I brought my photographer along, as I usually did and about 12 to 15 volunteers showed up. I provided hazmat suits, gloves, trashbags, and we cleaned the streets of the very dirty Tenderloin district for three hours, along with a Veteran's housing unit called *Swords to Plowshares. Swords to Plowshares* is an amazing Veteran's organization that provides job training, housing, and benefits advocacy to low income and homeless U.S. military veterans, but the square lot that their housing unit sits on was filled with piles of trash, food, diapers, and hypodermic needles. The veterans and owners of the housing unit were extremely grateful that we cleaned up their area, and the homeless folks and passersby on the streets also were very appreciative.

My volunteers and I after my San Francisco Day of Action, in front of the Swords to Plowshares veterans organization.

Another time, I happened to meet a couple while at a friend's apartment complex recreation room who were making signs for an upcoming protest. I asked them what the signs were for, and they told me it was for the new Assembly Bill 5 gig work bill that was going to be decided on soon. At the time I hadn't heard much about it, so I asked them lots of questions and learned all about the bill and why they were protesting it.

Two days later I joined them at their protest. I threw on jeans, grabbed a construction vest and a hard hat, made signs and marched along with them in the streets of San Diego. I talked to as many of the protesters as I could, dozens of them, and heard their personal stories and struggles over how this bill would impact their lives, their businesses, their families. Their pain became my pain, their plight became my plight. These were hard-working Americans all across the state who were about to be stripped of their livelihoods all because of a stupid bill spearheaded by careless, out-of-touch Democratic leaders who thought they somehow knew better than the actual workers being affected by it. Simply because I took the time to notice something, ask questions, listen, and join those in the trenches, I found another cause with which I connected that allowed me to champion for people and be their voice.

Protesting with many workers affected by Assembly Bill 5.

The homelessness problem is a huge topic in San Francisco and I talked about it a lot throughout my campaign. Many politicians "talked" about it, but no one ever seemed to propose any tangible solutions. Instead of just talking about it, I wanted to dive in and really understand the issue from the ground up. So, I hung out and talked to the actual homeless on the streets. I interviewed them. I asked them what their stories were and how they got to be living on the streets. I asked them what their biggest challenges were and what they needed that they weren't receiving that could help them and get them on the track to living a healthy and normal life again off the streets. I attended local city town halls and meetings that discussed the building of new "Navigation Centers," which were supposedly centers that navigate the homeless into the real world again. I talked to and got to know the people attending these meetings, so I could understand all sides and arguments of the entire homeless situation, which was multidimensional and not just a simple black and white issue.

Before I established my ground team, I walked back and forth on the streets of the farmers markets by myself waving my big campaign signs for weeks, even in the rain. I participated in as many rallies and protests as possible. This included not only the topics with which I agreed, but also topics I opposed, so I could understand the opposing viewpoint. I stopped getting my nails done halfway through my campaign, because I just didn't see the point! I was here to roll up my sleeves and work, and not just stand back and look pretty.

Action Items:

❏ Get in the habit of leading by example.

❏ Be someone who listens, faces problems head on, and dives in to try to solve them.

❏ Get in the habit of being someone who leaves environments better than when you arrive. If you see trash on the ground, pick it up. If you see something that needs attention, do it yourself or lead a group of people to join you.

❏ Adopt the mindset and habits of a servant, a person who works *FOR the people* and contributes positively to your community and country.

❏ Leave people better through your conversations.

❏ Be an example, and you will shine brightly. Everyone else will appear like dull pebbles in comparison.

CHAPTER 12

PREPARE FOR THE RINOS

"They knew they would throw every lie they could at me, and my family, and my loved ones. They knew they would stop at nothing to try to stop me. Nevertheless, I take all of these slings and arrows, gladly for you. I take them for our movement — so that we can finally take our country back."
— **Donald J. Trump**

When I decided to run for congress, I thought that I would be spending most of my time undoubtedly fighting my main enemies — Nancy Pelosi and the left. What I wasn't quite prepared for was that I would end up spending the majority of my time fighting the Establishment *RINOs* on my own side.

First, a little background on one of the (many) challenges in my particular election and race. In 2010, thanks to Proposition 14 and the foolish people that voted on it, the open "jungle primary" passed. California is one of only three states that employ this election process known as the jungle primary. This allows only the top two vote-getters of any party to move on to the general election. Normally, there is one top vote-getter of each party, so — whoever earns the most votes of the Republican candidates can move on to the general election, and whoever earns the most votes of the Democratic candidates moves on to the general election. Obviously, the incumbent is usually a guaranteed shoe-in. So, it was pretty expected that Nancy Pelosi would get enough votes to sail past the primary election and onto the general election, which only leaves room for *one* other candidate to make it through, from any party.

Also, if you're running in a tough blue district like I was, it is highly likely that another Democrat will make it through before a Republican does. This is why it was such a tough situation with my Republican opponent and I both competing in the same race — there was only room for one of us, if that, as we also were competing with the other three Democratic candidates in the race and we would be splitting the Republican vote with one another. It wasn't impossible for one of us to make it through to the general, but it was definitely much tougher than if just one of us Republicans were running.

My opponent, JD, represented what we often call the "Old Guard." A few months into the race, it became pretty clear that he was the choice that many of the Establishment members wanted. He was more "in the club," so to speak and I was the outsider. The more I got to know the political world, the more I understood that a large percentage of the higher-ups that are in control of the local and state GOP chapters tend to throw their support into the Old Guard brand of candidates or the Mitt Romney RINO type. They represent the status quo who are tame, politically correct, and really don't ruffle any feathers. The state GOPs often don't take a chance on the young, fresh, grassroots candidates who are more bold, boisterous, and openly "anti-Establishment." Obviously,

I speak my mind and don't necessarily "play by all the rules," which makes me attractive to many political folks, but sometimes riles up the old buttoned-up Establishment types. Unfortunately, these dynamics make getting elected all the more difficult for true, solid patriots with great hearts and abilities to make a serious impact in our country.

From day one, JD seemed to do everything he could to try to get me out of the race. He asked people to ask me if I would step down from the race. I did not. When that didn't work, he tried copying my great ideas, since he didn't seem to have any creativity and bright ideas of his own.

Since none of those things worked, he and his allies spent the majority of his campaign smearing me, attacking me, and pressuring me out of the race. Are you familiar with a tactic called the *"Wrap-up Smear?"* If you're not, you'll most certainly *get* familiar with it as you dive deeper into the political world. The Wrap-up Smear is a political tactic that Nancy Pelosi herself has actually admitted publicly that she and the Democrats frequently use — and we encounter it nearly every day whether you realize it or not. The tactic is also referred to in different terms in Saul Alinsky's infamous political playbook, *Rules for Radicals.* Particularly his fifth rule, *"Ridicule is man's most potent weapon."* As well as his 13th rule, *"Pick the target, freeze it, personalize it, and polarize it. Cut off the support network and isolate the target from sympathy."*

This is what the left successfully does to Donald Trump every day, since the beginning of his presidential campaign in 2016. They accuse him of something, usually false, then feed the false claim to "credible news outlets," such as the *New*

York Times or *The Washington Post* or MSNBC, and then those news outlets publish or broadcast stories about it. People then read or hear those stories and since it's reported by a "credible source," they believe the falsehoods to be true. Remember the infamous Trump "dirty dossier," or the ridiculous sexual harassment and "train" stories thrown at Judge Brett Kavanaugh? The Wrap-up Smear is responsible for convincing millions of otherwise intelligent people to believe that the president and all of his supporters are "racist," "misogynistic," and "Russian agents," and that Putin and Russian bots are responsible for "stealing" the election from Hillary Clinton.

These are the same Alinsky tactics that JD, Grease Ball, and their "gang" used on me throughout my campaign. And it is all the more despicable coming from people who claim to be on the same "Republican" side.

Marco took it upon himself to start co-managing JD's Twitter accounts, because old man RINO had hardly any social media following previously and had no idea how to use it. Since Marco had a huge social media following, he really helped grow JD's platform. Anything he could do to bolster up my opponent's campaign was a win for him in his vindictive mind.

Like vultures, they dug up any random bit of information or photos they could get their hands on or obtain from my ex's hacking and stalking "assistance" to use and spin into some wild tale. Of course they would never put any context to the things they posted or ask me to clarify the facts about them; they just fabricated their own silly context and storyline just like CNN and BuzzFeed do. Then, keeping true to Alinsky form, Mr. RINO paid a certain blogger, let's just call him "Andrew Parks," who manages a certain online blog, to further complete their Wrap-up Smear on me and make their falsehoods about me appear credible.

The little "gang" of JD, Grease Ball, Marco, and this media blogger worked together to co-author hit piece after hit piece on me to try to gain the upper hand and pressure me out of the race. I'm not going to drop the real name or website of this National Enquire-esque, poor excuse for a media outlet, as I don't want to give them any more traffic, but a decent amount of people read these articles, and a small percentage of the readers are gullible enough to actually believe them unfortunately. It wasn't some kind of conspiracy theory that JD and Marco were directly feeding and paying this vile propaganda artist to write about me. The information came directly from them and is also verified in the numerous payments JD made to Andrew Parks, documented in his FEC reports. And on top of that, his "Sponsored by John Dennis for Congress" ads were plastered right there on the top of the blogger's homepage during the campaign! I discovered that this blogger is known for politicians paying him to write nasty fake news pieces about their opponents to try to gain the upper hand in elections, so once you know that about him I would think it would be hard to read anything he says as credible. Then again, there are still somehow thousands of sheep who watch CNN!

Mr. RINO and the gang liked to peddle a false narrative they created that I was some kind of "criminal" and therefore he was the "squeaky clean candidate who was better fit for office." One of the things he smugly told people was that I had a DUI and a "criminal record." This is ridiculous fake news that actually makes me laugh. The extent of it? Back in the day when I was in college and 19 years old, I was at a Halloween party and had a — gasp! — beer on the sidewalk outside of the party with my friends. The little university cops on bikes broke up the party, gave me a ticket and slapped me with a Minor in Possession (MIP), which they gave out like candy to nearly everyone. My friend still has the picture of me dressed in my little bunny costume with floppy ears and a sad face as the cop is handing me my ticket. That's a very different thing though than a DUI and "criminal record." Oh and I apparently accidentally missed a court date for a traffic ticket that I had back when I was 20 or so, and I may have also bounced a check around the same age. Woooah, I'm such a big baaad criminal aren't I? I really don't have anything to explain or apologize about since these were so minor and so long ago, and I actually feel sorry for people like these pathetic old men who apparently didn't have any fun or get into a little harmless trouble in their young adulthood. As the great Honorable Brett Kavanaugh, world class survivor of the months-long smear-a-thon says, "Yeah, "I drank beer with my friends. I liked beer. I still like beer. So *what*?!"

There was also a ridiculous video of me that they dug up from about 10 years ago, where I was in a limo bus for a wine tasting tour in wine country with a group of friends and my boyfriend at the time. And what is inside most limo buses? Why yes, stripper poles! So yeah, in the video I'm dancing on the pole, having fun, fully clothed like everyone else in the group. I don't even know who took the video or how the heck it was unearthed, but the next thing I know, Mr. RINO is sending it out to hundreds of Republicans and people on social media, basically claiming how it's "proof" that I'm "wild and unfit for office."

Marco also created many fake Twitter, Instagram and Facebook accounts so he could flood my page with nasty comments, and even created profiles that looked identical to mine, impersonating me, but posting all defamatory tweets, pictures, and videos of me, along with their smear articles. Then the gang would all retweet each other so the info would circulate, and they would get off on it and pat each other on the backs like little schoolboys with nothing better to do. *Clap, Clap.* Cool story, bros.

More fake news: Then there was a picture they dug up on me from my personal Facebook from years ago and posted on their Twitter accounts. It was taken when I was living part-time in Dubai for business, and my friend and we wore the local hijab for a day as a little social experiment. "OMG look, DeAnna supports Islamic terrorists, too! She really should step down! Support John instead!" Give me a freaking BREAK. Talk about desperation.

The true story, however, was that the more popularity I garnered with my campaign, the more infuriated these guys were and the more they grasped at straws to try to take me down.

Fake Playboy: Oh this one was fun... my ex thought it would be real cute to take an old headshot of me, blow up my boobs real big so they looked fake, and then photoshop it onto some plug-and-play *Playboy* magazine template with the title "Rent DeAnna out for sale and Casino parties!" and pass it around claiming that I had done shoots for *Playboy*. "See, she's done *Playboy*, too! She's bad, you better pull your support for her! Vote for John Dennis instead!" It was so utterly pathetic. Of course I never did anything of the sort. Oh and just a handy hint gentlemen, if you're going to photoshop a pic onto something you may want to make it look a little more believable and remove all the traces of green screen there, buddies. **Eye-roll emoji.**

They did other crazy things too, like posted old email exchanges that my stalker had hacked into and obtained, they stalked my friends' Instagram accounts to hunt down and post old videos and pictures of me... any little thing that these greedy piranhas could get their hands on and exploit, they did. You'd think they would be focusing their time and energy on their own campaigns they were supposed to be running instead of obsessing over mine? Perhaps this is why these candidates keep running and losing. I dunno, just a thought!

For the record, I have heard from some political friends that Marco was also telling people that he had given me large sums of money, and he also gave me money or assistance for this book. That never happened, because I never accepted any payments from him, nor did I even think about writing a book up until a few months ago after my election when a publishing company approached me and pitched me the idea. Not to mention if I ever had. Not to mention if I ever had accepted any payments, he would have undoubtedly recorded evidence and published this information to make a big story of it because that's the kind of thing he does.

Thank God for my army of loyal digital soldiers! They had my back and fought off much of these attacks with their digital swords and might. As my social media following continued to grow, in time they were able to quickly identify fake sock accounts created by Marco and the gang and called them out. They were able to quickly spot attacks made by them, they defended me, and spread the word. I'm forever grateful for all the ways they helped me through the ups and downs of my campaign.

There were some days when I honestly thought about quitting. They would just smear me so hard and make it appear that the odds were so stacked against me that I felt exhausted and hopeless. I tried to just laugh off most of it and let it roll off my back, because it was such nonsense. However, probably the smear that really hurt was the rumor they kept spreading that I was some kind of promiscuous slut. Why were these old men, two married and one gay (not that there's anything wrong with that), even in any position to make claims about my private life and act like they knew me? It's despicable that I even had to defend myself over and over for something like this. It wasn't even just these old men that were saying these grotesque lies, it was also some of their women friends in the Conservative movement. The funny thing is, if they actually looked into my bedroom windows to get the truth, they would be very disappointed because they'd find it pretty damn boring with my lackluster personal life.

It also was highly ironic that the men and women who were going around saying I was a slut are individuals who do not know me personally whatsoever, and with whom I've never even had a single conversation. And worse, these are people who call themselves "Christians." Many of these people, including JD, even have young daughters. It's truly disgusting and shameful, and I just can't understand the behavior or mindset to be honest. Especially because we're all supposed to be on the same team, fighting a common enemy and fighting to take back America. That's where all our energy should be expended, not toward fighting each other.

It's also such a gross misrepresentation of my heart, my character, my goals in life and everything for which I stand. I want nothing more than to be married with a great husband and a family of my own. I long for it. Sorry JD, I do not have a cookie-cutter life, nor the wealth and white-picket fenced estate in one of the wealthiest areas of the country like you apparently do. Excuse me for being imperfect and born into a millennial generation that is ridden with obstacles to finding a quality partner and building a family. So, if you're a single woman or man, you just learn to make the best of the situation and there's nothing else to really do other than put your focus into career goals and hang out with friends while you're looking for your hubby or wife. I absolutely abhor the hypersexual hook-up culture. I don't do one-night stands. I believe sex is sacred and shouldn't be thrown around casually. And although I went through a brief, slightly more "Liberal" phase of my life in my early 20s and was moderately pro choice at one point, I later saw the error of those ways and I have come to be proudly pro-life. My entire book *Making Love Great Again* was about these very issues, if these people even bothered to read a page or two of it. I break down the problems with our modern culture and feminism, the sexual revolution, and how they've made us, especially my millennial generation, so corrupt and unhappy. I talk about the need for bringing Conservative values and faith in God back to the forefront. If more of us upheld Conservative values, as well as prioritized marriage and family over money, selfishness, and sex, I believe we would all be much happier and much better off as a country. All of this is part of my platform!

But no, they didn't care about my true feelings and practices — just like how the left doesn't care about finding or reporting the actual truth when it comes to Trump. They simply decided since I'm a woman, not yet married, and I don't look like a total troll, that I must be "promiscuous" — or, they would paint me as such regardless, because creating a false narrative was all they had to try to gain the upper hand and siphon attention away from me. It also really hurt since these people *knew very well* what I had been dealing with behind the scenes with Marco, they *knew* that he was making my life a living hell, yet they were all too happy to gang up with him and pile on the tormenting so JD could benefit.

Some days were really, really rough, to be honest. But then, miraculously, my survival instincts kicked in again and it became clear that I had to stay strong and keep fighting. The harder they tried to knock me down, and the uglier and nastier they got, the more convinced I became that I HAD to stay in the race. As time wore on, their true corrupt colors were revealing themselves more and more. I realized I just could not in good conscience allow a man like JD to lead the country and have our president's ear. These cronies also represented the textbook stereotype of what a lot of people have of Republicans, but they are actually the "Old Guard Republicans" — elitist, judgmental, pretending to be holier than thou and better than everyone else — while in actuality they are often the biggest hypocrites! The "Old Guard" of yesteryear is what we want gone and replaced with compassionate new blood that can truly make a positive impact in America.

Another fearless friend of mine, Erin Cruz, has run for California Senate against Dianne Feinstein, and is currently running for Congress in California's 36th congressional district after winning her primary this year. She's had to deal with her fair share of nasty Swamp monsters, and even wrote a book detailing her battles against them in *Crushing Corruption: Draining the California Swamp*. Here's what she had to say about these kinds of corrupt Establishment players:

"Conservatives, Republicans are largely faith-based as a whole. The majority of those I have met are in fact genuine, more often than not you can see the display of their faith in their everyday interactions with others and approach to politics. Then there are those who are not genuine, and use their "Christian faith" as a heavy stick to attack others or sway votes and support. This was the case with one of my Republican opponents in my race for Senate. I have never witnessed someone use God and everything we as Christians of faith hold sacred to tear another apart in the way he did, and publicly. In addition, the whole 'I am more Christian than Erin Cruz' approach was definitely disturbing. This man was like a weasel and approached me with clear intentions, — to insult, intimidate, and cause nothing but division and trouble. There was a stench, figuratively speaking. It really woke me up to how far people will go just to buy a vote. Selling their souls to greed, ego, and for personal gain. A lot of these Establishment Swamp creatures completely lack authenticity, unfortunately. This is the exact opposite of what we need. In fact, often, if someone states that they've been in business for 40 years this would be an impressive accomplishment. But, in this Swamp monster's case, as is the case with many others, it was all just posturing, fluffing, and putting on a show in an

attempt to gain ground. Over my career and years of political activism, I have met so many accomplished professionals, as I'm sure you have — be it in academia or in their respective trades. Don't measure the man by his wallet or title. Many of the most brilliant minds, who have literally transformed the world, often don't have the fancy degrees or titles or the "perfect" pedigree. The best messengers are often imperfect, in fact, while those who boast about being the most flawless are often the most flawed. A brilliant and talented mind must not be wasted. Weasels of the world, I have learned they are takers, not actually givers who add value to the community and the world. Be aware and grow your knowledge of what each looks like!"

★ ★ ★

A Target on My Back

It was always one thing after another. It is accurate to say I feel like I went through a literal war, because not only was I running a campaign against the most high-profile individual in the United States second to President Trump, but I was fighting constant attacks from both my stalker *and* my RINO opponent who were working in cahoots — all while trying to keep a brave and confident face. Everything for which I worked so hard in my life seemed to be getting torn down. I was working relentlessly, putting myself out there and getting filleted every day just to serve my country, but it almost felt like I was being punished for it.

Everywhere I went, my stalker would somehow track and locate me within hours and start threatening and extorting me again from new phone numbers and many different aliases. It got to a point where I couldn't even share exciting things happening in my campaign or reveal when I was going to appear in the news, because my stalker and opponent would be hot on my trail trying to ruin it. It was really sick. Every time I would take one step forward and celebrate an accomplishment, I would get knocked down again by Marco or Mr. RINO and his team.

I was so excited one morning in the fall at the beginning of my campaign when I woke up, checked my email, and there it was — an email from "FOX & Friends" inviting me to do an "exclusive" interview about my run against Nancy Pelosi! It was perfect timing because it was the week before the SF Day of Cleanup I was about to hold. This was going to be so great for my campaign. I talked to the producers on the phone and triple confirmed everything. My team and I were jumping for joy. I only shared the news with my inner circle and my campaign Twitter group. I wrote up my talking points and spent the whole night rehearsing. I laid out my fabulous pink dress, jewelry, and heels for the morning. I looked in the mirror and said to myself, "This is it! This is going to be an epic marker in my campaign that I'll always remember."

Someone from my Twitter group made a tweet late that night that I was going to be on "FOX and Friends." I was a little apprehensive about sharing that on Twitter, but I kept it there. I could barely go to sleep, because I was so excited and the car they had for me was scheduled to pick me up at the wee hour of 3 am. After managing to get about an hour and a half sleep I was up again, got ready, and anxiously awaited in my pretty pink dress by my front door for the car to pick me up. Ten minutes went by after the scheduled time. Nothing. Then 20 minutes went by, and still nothing. I knew something had to be wrong. I called the producer to let them know the car was running late. She checked with the other producers to see what was happening and to my shock she came back and said, "Oh, we're sorry, the segment has been cancelled." My jaw dropped.

I couldn't get any real answers as to why the abrupt cancellation, and they gave me no date for a rescheduled segment. I was devastated! I had a strong hunch as to what may have happened, but I didn't want to believe it. I didn't want to believe that this person was that evil.

I later got confirmation that my hunch was right — it was apparently Marco and JD and the gang who had somehow managed to get my segment cancelled. Since Marco was always stalking my accounts, as soon as he saw the tweet about my upcoming interview on FOX and Friends, he evidently told JD's team who are chummy with a higher-up at FOX and had the power to get my segment axed. *So dirty!* I could not get back on FOX for the rest of my campaign, until the very end, and it was very frustrating. But alas, that's the muddy, dirty RINO Swamp for ya.

Cheers and Smears

Man, someone should've warned me to wear a wetsuit for all the smears! Towards the beginning of my campaign in the Fall, I had organized a big campaign kick-off rally on the steps of City Hall in San Francisco, as another means of building local support and staking my flag into the ground as the woman taking on Nancy Pelosi who was going to help restore sanity to the district. I was so excited to have my friend, the great Warren Farrell as my keynote guest speaker to kick off the rally for me, because he and I both champion Fathers' rights and the family unit. But because of my past experience with this jealous little gang trying to tear down my events, I was anxious about posting my flyers announcing my guest. I waited till about a week before the rally to finally reveal the identity of him, and my supporters were super excited to see him once they found out. The speaker and I confirmed, double confirmed, and triple confirmed over the course of a month, because I didn't want to have any issues.

Then, the week of the rally, Marco started blowing up my phone again with threats and messages, telling me that he, Grease Ball, and JD were contacting my guest speaker and working to pressure him into cancelling. He sent me screenshots of Ferrell's phone numbers he had tracked down to show me he was serious. I honestly didn't think Farrell would cancel, especially since we had talked about the event so much and he knew how important it was to me that he was there. However, sure enough, two days before the rally, he sent me a rather vague email telling me that he would not be able to speak due to the power outages that had been going on in San Francisco at the time, which he said had thrown off his work schedule. I don't know for sure if his reason for backing out at the last minute was legitimate, or if Marco and JD really had been successful at pressuring him into cancelling. But it was another disappointing hit regardless. Nevertheless, I persisted.

Then came the actual day of my rally. It was a beautiful day on the steps of City Hall in San Francisco, I had practiced my riveting campaign speech a hundred times, and had a substantial number of supporters show up. Which is a difficult thing to do in general, but even more of an accomplishment as a young Republican who was fresh on the scene in Communist San Francisco running against their beloved god Nancy Pelosi.

But the little gang just couldn't let me have one moment of glory. As I started delivering my speech and rallied up the crowd, I saw creepy Grease Ball sneak into the crowd with his tall, lanky stature and snakey energy, going around talking to all of my people one by one while handing them something. Then he started talking pretty intensely to the news reporters who were there for me. What on earth was he doing and saying? I continued through my speech and tried not to let it distract or bother me, even though I could see him spreading his vitriol in my peripheral vision. After I finished to a cheering crowd, I stepped down to see what exactly he was up to. It turned out he was passing around flyers to everyone, with a "Paid for by John Dennis for Congress" stamp on them that had a picture of me with the word "fake" written across it in red. They also typed up bullet points on why I was a "bad candidate," why JD was the better candidate to support, and again, alluded to me as a "criminal" and "promiscuous." (Me screaming silently in my head again, *BEEEER when I was in College! And I haven't even dated anyone in many months!!*)

He continued to hover around, spoke to all my supporters, and aggressively tried to strong-arm the news reporters to stop interviewing me on their network and start giving JD interviews instead. One of the reporters, who was getting irritated with his pressuring, finally asked, "Well if this John Dennis guy is such a great candidate, then why isn't he here? Why isn't he holding a campaign rally of his own?" Ding Ding Ding! So instead of JD putting in the hard work to organize a campaign kick-off rally of his own, which he never did in all his five times running for public office, he sat in his gated estate like a lazy coward and sent his creepy campaign manager to mine to try to heckle and ruin it. It's literally something that a leftist would do to a conservative!

But again, I held my head up high, stayed focused, and went on with the show. They wanted me to get discouraged. They wanted me to get deflated over their shenanigans and lose heart, but I wouldn't let them get the best of me. I'm a fighter and I was determined to keep my fire ablaze and continue my fight.

This is the Bible verse I would pray almost daily to get me through the toughest and darkest times:

Ephesians 6:10-18 New International Version (NIV)

The Armor of God

"Finally, be strong in the Lord and in his mighty power. Put on the full armor of God, so that you can take your stand against the devil's schemes. For our struggle is not against flesh and blood, but against the rulers, against the authorities, against the powers of this dark world and against the spiritual forces of evil in the heavenly realms. Therefore put on the full armor of God, so that when the day of evil comes, you may be able to stand your ground, and after you have done everything, to stand. Stand firm then, with the belt of truth buckled around your waist, with the breastplate of righteousness in place, and with your feet fitted with the readiness that comes from the gospel of peace. In addition to all this, take up the shield of faith, with which you can extinguish all the flaming arrows of the evil one. Take the helmet of salvation and the sword of the Spirit, which is the word of God."

★ ★ ★

Taking Out the Trash

Remember the "San Francisco Day of Action" I held early on in my campaign to clean up the streets of the city? Well when I announced it, it drummed up a lot of enthusiasm and support, especially because the president kept putting San Francisco's dirty streets on the news. Many local people RSVP'd to the cleanup. Even the Republican candidate running for mayor at the time, "Anne," was excited about it and wanted to get involved. She posted it up on Eventbrite and Meetup.com sites, sent out email blasts, and promoted it on her social media sites, gathering a lot of RSVPs. However, a few people were apparently not so excited to clean up the district.

Immediately when I announced that I was leading the cleanup, the jealous hater that JD is, started *trashing* it to everyone, saying it was a stupid idea. Since he was so out of touch and not a part of the original MAGA movement like I am, he also didn't even know who Scott Presler was at that time and had never heard of his famous city cleanup events.

But, he went from mocking my cleanup, to copying me and announcing he was going to lead a cleanup himself once he realized the idea of a city cleanup was gaining traction. It was aggravating of course, but all l could do was ignore him and focus on planning my upcoming event. Well, just two days before my big cleanup day, my friend, Anne, who was running for Mayor, and who was partnering with me for the cleanup, suddenly texted me, saying "I'm sorry, but I have to cancel and cannot come to the cleanup anymore."

I knew something was sketchy, especially given that she was so excited to partner with me on it up until that night. Anne also abruptly cancelled the event on her Eventbrite and Meetup.com pages and with no explanation, so many of the people who had RSVP'd were led to believe that it had been cancelled altogether and didn't know I was still holding it without her, rain or shine. I called Anne and tried to figure out why she suddenly cancelled, although I already had a hunch why she did. Anne finally admitted that she was "heavily pressured" to cancel the event and back out of any further support for me. I kept digging, but she wouldn't say anything more — only that she couldn't say and she would not come.

I came to find out later that my hunch was right as usual — it was JD and Grease Ball who had "heavily pressured" her into cancelling her support for me and my cleanup day. Those dirty dogs apparently even made a "trade" with her — if she cancelled all her support and relationship with me moving forward, then they would throw her a bone and JD would give her an "endorsement" shout-out on Twitter and have the SF GOP support her a bit in the final few weeks of her mayoral campaign.

Prior to this, JD and the SF GOP spent their entire campaign year either ignoring Anne or ridiculing her, and not giving her an ounce of their support. They thought she was obnoxious and too bold in her unabashed support for Trump and the MAGA agenda. We found out later that Mr. RINO and

Grease Ball had also "heavily pressured" other people to back out of coming to my cleanup as well, in an effort to try to embarrass me with a low turnout, so they could spread it around to everyone.

So, that rather than acting like a classy, mature leader who is supposed to be the chairman of the local GOP, and joining another Republican in doing something positive for the district — at a time when President Trump put San Francisco on blast for its public trash crisis — JD stooped so low as to pressure people *out of* coming and... picking up *trash*. Absolutely petty and childish. And, he's twice my age.

As if they couldn't get any more trashy, RINO also sent Grease Ball to show up to my cleanup, lurking and following me around everywhere as usual while sneaking pictures and videos of me. I asked him if he wanted to throw on a HazMat suit and participate in the cleanup, and he refused. I asked him if I could help him with anything and he said "nope." I asked him why exactly he was there if he wasn't going to join the cleanup or talk to me, and he said "just to watch you and document everything." Of course he was. He actually made my volunteers and I quite uncomfortable, because he just creeped around following us for a longtime sneaking pictures and videos while we were dealing with sensitive materials and hypodermic needles. Immediately after the cleanup, he sent his photos to "Andrew The Blogger" to write up another fake news narrative that he published the next day, saying "How embarrassing, no one showed up to DeAnna's cleanup!" and, "There was not enough trash at DeAnna's cleanup, how stupid!" It's exactly like what the left constantly does to the president — showing a picture of a rally before anyone's even arrived and publishing a story, like: "Empty Stadium at

Trump's Rally!" And, whenever he tries to do something positive, they put a negative spin on it: "Trump provides coronavirus tests, but there aren't enough people taking the test!" I couldn't believe these were fully grown men acting this way.

Some of my campaign team members who were present encouraged me to write up a formal complaint email about Grease Ball's unprofessional behavior and send to the SF GOP and the CAGOP just to have it on record (which again, just highlights the problematic conflict of interest, since all complaints and directives go through JD himself as he is the chairman and Grease Ball is the executive director!). Rather than listening to it with any sincerity or fairness though, the complaint was just laughed off and totally minimized by JD and Grease Ball. Then the day after that, Andrew the Blogger published yet another hit piece about me, *mocking my formal email t*o the GOP. They even published my actual email — what was supposed to be an internal and private email — in the public article. So if you send any private email or have a phone conversation to the internal higher-ups of the SF GOP, apparently it's fair game for them to publish your internal memos in the next day's public news? Just for a few LOLZ? I mean who does that? Are we in Junior High?

Brr... a Cold and Very "Uninviting" Holiday Season

In December 2019, I was invited by a friend and supporter to attend the local Republican Women's Christmas Party. I was looking forward to attending, though a bit trepidatious, because the head of this organization is Jan, an older woman who is one of JD's allies. She has been one of the older ladies saying nasty things about me to other people, even though we had never even had a conversation. Nevertheless, I heard she broke her hip, so I was planning on bringing her a poinsettia and a card as a token of friendship and good will. I really wanted to attend to continue demonstrating to the community that I am serious about wanting to establish relationships with them and be an active part of the community. My friend did not tell this woman yet that I was going to be his guest, because he was well aware of her unkind behavior toward me.

The day before the party, my friend called me and said that Jan demanded he tell her who his guest was. When he finally told her it was me, she angrily scoffed at him and told him I was not welcome to the party. "If you even try to come with her, neither of you will be welcomed in," she said. She told him she would refund his tickets, because she was that adamant about me not coming. This old woman who didn't even know my personal life even had the nerve to call me a "floozy" and other choice words. Little old me? I was disgusted, but not necessarily shocked. How's that for a leader of a large women's Republican organization for welcoming Republicans and new members into the fold? No wonder their youngest member is like 50.

This is the kind of juvenile, vicious behavior coming from JD's team and others in the "Establishment" side of the GOP that I was running up against constantly throughout my campaign. This kind of behavior is exactly why many good, anti-Establishment, grassroots patriots are blocked from ever getting elected into Congress while Establishment swamp creatures continue to get elected and roam freely. The *glass ceiling* for patriots is very real and that's why it's ever essential that we continue to fight that status quo. I'm not alone — I have many other awesome patriot friends who ran for office or are currently running, and have faced the same kind of nasty attacks and resistance from the Establishment GOP. And my goodness, look at what Trump went through? Look at what he continues to go through. The Swamp runs deep — and we must defeat it!

Meanwhile, I figured the best revenge was just to stay focused like a racehorse, keep dominating with creative ideas and remain front and center with a winning attitude. My following continued to grow, grow, grow, and so did my influence and popularity along with it.

CHAPTER 13

HIGH VISIBILITY:

HOW TO MASTER YOUR MEDIA AND PUBLICITY GAME

"Small stars still light up big skies."
— **Matshona Dhliwayo**

★ ★ ★

When you run for public office, you've got to be *visible!* You must be seen and heard — ongoingly. Here's another rule of mine: when you run for office, you give up the right to be a homebody.

You must be out and about circulating with people. When you're not circulating with people in person, you are active on social media and doing interviews on the mainstream media. If you're more shy and introverted, running your campaign will be a great and necessary breakthrough in overcoming your shyness.

Become an Event Energizer Bunny

I tried to speak at as many events as possible, no matter how small or large. If groups or organizations aren't inviting you to speak, then reach out and ask them. Even if they can squeeze you in for two minutes to talk in advance of a featured speaker, it's a success. The more you speak, the more polished you'll become, and the more people will know your name and mission.

Go to as many events in your district as possible so people see your face and you start getting recognized. Running a campaign is not for the lazy. They don't call it "running" a campaign for nothing! You should be aware of all the events in your city every week. If there are big events outside your district as well that you can attend, I strongly encourage you to go.

Use the News to *Become* the News

You and your campaign team should be scouring the news every morning, and be on top of the latest news and trending topics throughout the day. Always take advantage of current events to get yourself in the news cycle. Anytime there is a hot trending topic in the news, put out your comments and public statements about it on your social media platforms. Publish a press release with your statements about the topic, and then send the talking points and press releases to your target media outlets, both locally and nationally. Try to have original comments, even controversial or a bit provocative, because that's what grabs the attention of the public and the media.

Making noise with the media (One America News Network).

Think about it this way: a media outlet or reporter is going to call on *someone* to comment and weigh in on any given trending news topic. If a news outlet will be calling on an expert to be interviewed, it might as well be *you!* You certainly don't want it to be your opponent — and that's why you need to beat them to the chase.

Here are just some examples of prime opportunities I took to stay in the news cycle:

- **Impeachment:** When Nancy was constantly in the news for leading the charge of the sham impeachment hearings, who better to weigh in on this than the top candidate running against her for Congress? I made sure it was me, of course.

- **Homelessness and trash:** When Trump first put the spotlight on San Francisco for drowning in homelessness, feces, trash, and crime, I jumped at the opportunity to weigh in on the crisis and lend myself as an expert to the media. It prompted me to organize cleanups in the city. I created video ads regarding the cleanups that went viral, and talked about how Nancy spends all her time obsessing over impeaching the president rather than fixing the growing problems in her own district. This became a continuous battle cry throughout my campaign. It earned me a lot of publicity and interviews all year.

- **Gender Equality Act:** Whenever Nancy talks about the Gender Equality Act, I comment and send talking points out to the media exposing the malicious underbelly of the act and explain how the seemingly benevolent act actually will do much more harm to women and our culture than good.

- **Ripping up the SOTU:** When Nancy ripped up the State of the Union behind the president's back on national TV, it was all anyone could talk about for a month. Of course I predicted the tidal wave of media that would ensue and immediately took action to respond and became one of the leading "experts" to weigh in on it for weeks. I'll share more details with you on the "disciplinary action" I took in a later chapter.

- **Tara Reade accusation:** When the story of Tara Reade's accusations against Joe Biden started circulating the news, I knew it was going to be a major issue. I also had an intuitive feeling that the left would try to push it under the rug and expose their major hypocrisy with the #MeToo movement. So, I talked about it very vocally, published videos about it, and wrote an Op-Ed — called *"#MeToo has been exposed as* *the fraudulent political weapon it always was"* — that was published in several media outlets including, *The Western Journal* and *LifeZette*

How to master your speeches and interviews like a badass:

- **Bring as much FIRE and energy as possible:** get noticed and steal the whole show! The last thing you want to do is put people to sleep like Sleepy Joe Biden or Low Energy Jeb. You want to strut in there, be noticed, and wake the sleeping people up!

- **Don't blend into the walls, *OWN the room:*** at the start of your speech, the first phrase out of your mouth should be loud and energetic. Then you "set the stage" for people to pay attention to you. Your goal is to wake up the room. Shock and awe them. Do not let their eyes glaze over. Command their attention by speaking loud and vibrantly. Don't blend into the walls, *OWN the room!* My goal is to always be the most energetic of all other speakers.

- **Ask an opening question:** another great way to get the audience engaged is to start your talk by asking a question, or asking them to do something that immediately gets them moving and raises their energy.

My favorite openers are: *"Helloooo patriots! Now first I have a question for you. Raise your hand if you LOVE America! Raise your hand if you LOVE our president! Raise your hand if* *you can't stand Nancy Pelosi!"* Undoubtedly, people will excitedly wake up and raise their hands enthusiastically.

Another favorite is: *"Okay the first thing I want you to do if it's true for you is on the count of three, get up out of your chair and yell "I love America!"* This gets people out of their sleepy state and excited. Then when I continue, they pay attention.

Throughout my talks I ask the audience additional questions that keep them alert. I also tailor my talking points to my audience to predict what to say that will resonate with the hearts and minds of the attendees, based on the crowd. I love to throw political correctness out the window and say bold things that may sound a little provocative so they get that I'm someone who speaks the truth and tells it like it is. Don't be vanilla — be a Neapolitan Sundae with cherries on top.

- **Try not to read from a script:** reading from a script loses attention, it's boring, and feels inauthentic. Know your main messages well and speak from the heart with passion — it will resonate better with people. You may have to look at notes occasionally, but really try to memorize your best points and make eye contact with people in your audience from the right, to the center, to the left. It's also ideal to get out from the podium and walk around the stage so you keep people engaged. This is not a time to be meek or soft-spoken. Own your POWER and shine! Remember, when you speak passionately from the heart, people focus less on the exact words and more on the emotions that you stir up and they will remember you more for that. Think about how President Trump speaks. He speaks in memorable soundbites and catchphrases, wears his signature red tie, speaks loudly and energetically, and likes to go off script, speaking from the heart. This gives people the feeling that he's honest and trustworthy. Compare him to Jeb Bush or Pete Buttigeig who always give me the feeling that they are used car salesmen reading from scripts written by slick speechwriters.

- **Leave on a high note:** sometimes I must address negative topics, that are challenges in America or the district that I'm addressing in my campaign. However, I always like to end the talk or interview with a positive statement that leaves people feeling empowered, inspired, and confident that I am the right woman for the job that can lead them to victories. I also like to leave them with a feeling of hope and possibility. Never leave your audience feeling dull, depressed, or awkward.

Think about how President Trump always ends his rallies: *"Together, we will make America safe again. We will make America strong again. And together, we will make America great again."*

Speaking at an event in Newport Beach, CA.

Special Tips on Mastering TV and Phone Interviews

Plan and prepare what you want to talk about, and then stick to those talking points. Often news pundits will head in different directions or ask questions you had not anticipated. Most interviews are very short and you may not even get to address your top items. I learned the art of pivoting in interviews, so I can effectively answer the question they ask, yet get back to my key topics I most want to talk about.

For instance, in so many of my interviews, I was prepared and excited to talk about a new, specific topic in the news. But nine times out of 10, the interviewer started off by asking me about all the trashiness and homelessness in San Francisco. By the time I got through discussing the trash and piles of crap issue, we ran out of time and I didn't even get to weigh in on the main issue I was excited to talk about. So, after a few times this happened to me, I learned the art of "pivoting." The following is an example:

"Well, we all know that San Francisco has turned into a hellhole and has tons of trash and feces on the streets, but what is really important right now is... how Pelosi is handling this whole impeachment sham and what the implications are for Americans."

ALWAYS Be Prepared to Speak and Shine

When you are campaigning, people are going to approach you and opportunities will come at you unexpectedly. Be prepared to speak and shine, always look your best, be prepared for your elevator pitch with anything you feel you might need to put yourself at ease so you can shine.

To Recap:

❏ Get your business cards and campaign brochures produced right away in your campaign. They should be one of the first things you spend money on. You'll need plenty of cards and brochures with you at all your events, speaking engagements, and just out and about.

❏ REMEMBER: When running for public office, you give up the right to be a hermit, so circulate out and about.

❏ Be everywhere, speak everywhere, and attend as many events as possible.

❏ Take advantage of current events, trending topics, and hashtags to get yourself in the news cycle. Then, create a specific policy, act, or plan that is unique to you that addresses a certain problem that is specific to your voters that you can address frequently in the media and public.

CHAPTER 14

BE A FORCE TO BE RECKONED WITH

"To know your Enemy, you must become your Enemy."
— Sun Tzu

T he louder your voice and the bigger the threat you are, the harder [they] will attack and smear you.

Make sure your opponents know right off the bat that you are not a pushover and they can't mess with you! I tried to be polite and play nice in the sandbox. I tried to get "them" (JD and certain members of the "Establishment") to like me and treat me fairly. I tried to go the classy route and follow Reagan's rule of *"thou shall not talk poorly of a fellow Republican."* However, they just wanted to keep being nasty and playing dirty. I eventually decided, I'm here to be a wrecking ball to corruption in all forms. I'm not only going to take down Pelosi, I'm going to slay the RINOs and expose *anyone* corrupt in my path. It was time to throw the gloves off and start treating them like the hostile enemies they had become. My only regret is not fighting back harder, sooner.

When it came to the battle with Marco, I had to call the police so many times, I knew many of the officers by name. I was forced to file a Contempt of Court motion for his ongoing violation of the restraining order, and even called his attorney, closest friends, and family members to try to get them to intervene and stop his madness. He was making my life such a living hell that it was hard to focus much of the time. No matter how much I tried to reason with him or block him, his gangstalking, harassment, and extortion persisted.

Then, after many sleepless paranoid nights playing Whack-a-Mole with his attacks, I finally stopped giving a damn. I declared that I no longer was willing to be a hostage, and I broke free. '*I will no longer be a hostage. I will no longer be a hostage,*' I kept repeating to myself. '*I am a strong woman, I have faith and whatever he's going to throw at me, I will get through this and I can handle it.*'

Then came the mass messaging blasts that he had been threatening to send. Private emails from my past with no context were being published on social media. A "flash drive of information" was supposedly given to my opponent to use however he wished. Then the horror when I woke up one morning and realized that fully nude pictures of me were mass emailed and sent to apparently all of my contacts on Telegram and Instagram, and who knows where else. *Aaaaaah.*

Apparently they also were sent to several news outlets and reporters. To this day I have no idea who all has seen my bare body, and which of my colleagues may be too polite to tell me they have. I just kept praying for strength, and dusted myself off, fought through the embarrassment, and I am blessed to still be standing.

Then he started getting so desperate that he began making stupid mistakes severe enough to finally get caught by law enforcement. He texted me the home addresses of some of my family members he had obtained, along with promises to go after them and even send *Antifa* after them. (Who DOES that?!) He even threatened to call in terrorist threats to my little cousin Ross's upcoming wedding in New Jersey, for which he somehow was able to obtain the address and details.

His death threats to me and my family became more serious and frequent. "I can hire some guy on the streets to kill you for only $25,000," he texted me. "If you don't get back together with me I'm going to keep following you wherever you go and I'm going to turn into Dexter," he'd say. "I'm going to take you and your family out and I will be smiling in jail knowing a b*tch like you doesn't exist anymore in the world."

Then one night, after having a surprisingly really nice time at a Log Cabin Republican Christmas party, I came back to the new apartment. Only to find out that he had flown up from Los Angeles and had been waiting for me outside in the middle of the night, dressed in all black after blowing up my phone all week with crazy death threats.

I called the police, and they came down quickly and arrested him after finding he was in violation of an active restraining order and charged him with a number of felonies including criminal threats, attempted extortion, and aggravated stalking. I felt all sorts of emotions after they took him away, from fear, to guilt and relief. This should have never happened. All I wanted was for both of us to be living our lives in peace. But I finally fell to my knees and prayed.

He has been kept in custody since December as he was deemed a "threat to public safety" by the judges, and at the time that this book is going to print, we were still awaiting the trial to see if he would be convicted of his charges. I'm definitely scared, since many of his threats and violations had been electronic or through the many different phone numbers and aliases he used, and it's a possibility that he will be released from custody due to Coronavirus situations. I pray that God and the justice system determine the best solution, and one that is fair and compassionate, but also keeps me safe. This individual is relatively young and had a bright future ahead of him in the political world, so it honestly makes me upset that he put himself in this position. I never wanted for this to happen, but I was no longer safe and my life is valuable, too.

I share this story with you not as an attempt to gain any sort of sympathy or empathy from anyone. I am not a victim or want to be treated as such. But, just to share with you the good, bad, and ugly of my journey, because I promised you I would.

You can learn from my lessons and be careful who you date, be careful with whom you start relationships or even new friendships. Take it slow and go through a period of vetting them — or have friends vet them — before getting more serious.

Going through this experience also validated my feelings of frustration with the left for deploying what is probably their most harmful political weapon of all: the #MeToo Movement. The #MeToo Movement could have been really helpful, if it had been sincere and managed carefully. But the left appeared to create it purely as a political weapon to take down powerful men — specifically Conservative men. They used women as attack dogs to go after whichever target they wanted taken down next, and trained women to persecute men and #BelieveAllWomen, even when there were baseless accusations and no facts or evidence shared. Many false accusations have ensued and encouraged an onslaught of women who have cried #MeToo over a harmless joke or sex that was mutual at the time, but 20 years later they suddenly decided it wasn't. And who has gotten hurt the most from what the left has done with this movement? Not "Republicans." Not "Democrats." But REAL victims of sexual assault, harassment, and domestic violence behaviors. People hardly ever believe them anymore, because "wolf" has been cried so many times. Just like with claims of "racism," which has been completely watered down by the left overusing it, claims of harassment also have lost credibility and it's a horrible thing not to be believed in situations like these.

Living in the lawless Sanctuary Cities of San Francisco and Los Angeles while at the same time enduring the stalking situation also elucidated for me why we absolutely need the Second Amendment, and the ability for all states to allow open or concealed carry. We need to be able to protect ourselves, especially women, who are alone. This right shall never be infringed. I've never carried any weapons with me, nor have owned any, but now I'm in the process of taking firearm training and obtaining my Concealed Carry Permit. This experience also validates why we need the *police*, and why should never, ever entertain the idea of defunding or disbanding them! If it weren't for the *police* coming, and fast, who knows where I would be.

★ ★ ★

Daggers and Dynamite

The "endorsement meeting" of the SF GOP was really nothing but a crony rigged clown show, with JD and Grease Ball pulling the puppet strings. Remember how I keep mentioning the conflict of interest with John Dennis being both the chairman of the local GOP while at the same time running for the congressional seat for the district? Well, it all came to a head at the "endorsement meeting," in January this year, to determine which one of us Republican Congressional candidates for the race against Nancy would get the official Republican "endorsement" from the San Francisco GOP... chaired by John Dennis. JD made sure that every person showed up to the meeting, so there would be more than enough votes for him. He and Grease Ball also heavily pressured everyone for months to vote for him over me for the endorsement. It definitely put the group members in a precarious situation since he was the person facilitating the meeting, as well as both the chairman *and* a candidate asking the group for the endorsement. Many group members were understandably afraid of the repercussions of voting for me for the endorsement, against JD while he's staring at them in the face with the gavel in his hand, knowing they will have to face him after for as long as they're in the group.

JD and the other group leaders had me get up and give my endorsement pitch first. Honestly, I do not get awkward, uncomfortable, or nervous easily, but that was one of the most uncomfortable moments of my entire campaign. It was unbelievably unnerving having to give my endorsement "pitch" while staring at my enemy, JD, right across from me with his gavel in hand, and all of his "Team JD" allies on either side of him who made me feel so unwelcome for months. The tension in the room was so thick you could cut it with a machete. When they opened up the group for questions, JD had his allies asked me stupid "gotcha" questions, to try to make me as uncomfortable as possible and throw me off my game. However, I was prepared for their worst, and I stood my ground and weathered the storm.

He had his little pet, Jan, ask me questions regarding "information about my past," that was taken straight from their salacious hit pieces that they paid for and co-authored. Jan couldn't even hide the smug smirk on her face when she piped up and asked, "So, I heard many years ago that you got caught with a DUI, and that you also bounced a check — what do you have to say about that?"

I snapped back calmly, but strongly with, "First of all, Jan, you know damn well that this is a lie, and that it's one of many lies that were part of a coordinated smear campaign that the chairman of this group who's sitting right next to you, co-authored and funded, along with Clint, Andrew Parks, and my ex, Marco, who John has been working closely with. And secondly, there was never any DUI; it was a ticket I got while in college for having a beer outside of a Halloween party, which is completely different, and you know that." At that point, Jan and another snarky woman yelled, "Well, it was still wrong and you shouldn't be doing that when you're underage!" To which I quipped back, "Well if you've never had a drink in your life or had any fun when you were young Jan, I feel sorry for you, but I have nothing to apologize for and we all know who created these ridiculous stories anyway."

When I finished my pitch and went back to my seat, one of the group members whispered to me, "That was brave. The fact that you even showed up to this meeting knowing that it was going to be a horror show with all the cards stacked against you speaks to your bravery."

Then, it was Mr. RINO's turn to leave his Chairman's seat to get up in front of the room and give his endorsement speech for the Congressional seat. They were predictably totally light with him, but when they opened it up to Q&A, I felt it within my right to ask *him* some honest questions — about his past and *present*. So, I fired away. I pointed out the fact that he already ran for office four times and lost, and how he has proven to be a "losing" candidate, not a winner capable of making a dent against Nancy Pelosi. Then came the killer — I asked him if it was true that he and Grease Ball were still working and colluding with my ex, even while he was sitting in custody, in order to continue undermining my campaign. Boy, he didn't see that one coming! The whole room fell silent.

It was a little awkward while he and his allies scoffed and stared at me with daggers, but I didn't care anymore. These people treated me like absolute crap for months and never gave me any fair shake. They gossiped and spread fake news about me with each other, but never even cared to have a conversation with me or ask me questions to my face. This was war, and my gloves were off.

His answer was very telling: he fidgeted a lot, stuttered, turned red, evaded the question, talked in circles, and then, answered a different question. He never actually answered the question I asked. One woman in the group who's an ally of his jumped out of her seat and yelled "Hey, stop it! You are totally out of line!" But I fought back. "Why? You all asked questions about my personal life and past, why can't I ask him a question about his personal life and *present*?" After JD's squeamish and cringy meltdown, he stormed angrily back to his chair, huffing and puffing, and regained his gavel with a scowl.

Fortunately, my photographer was present that night, as usual, and filmed the whole meeting, so he put together a clip of what transpired. JD wasn't too happy that we filmed and posted the videos, but we sure were. :)

Of course when it came time for the group to vote on which candidate they wanted to give the endorsement to, most of the hands in the group were raised for JD (while he stared at them one by one in the face), which was expected. A few brave group members stuck to their guns and raised their hand for my endorsement; while several others told me privately that they were all set to vote for me, but chickened out at the last minute when faced with him staring at them intimidatingly. I don't really blame them though — they were the ones who would have to bear the wrath of JD for the rest of the year!

Even though JD "won" the endorsement of his own SF GOP group, of which he was the chairman, the fact that I showed up and went through the agonizing meeting was still an accomplishment for me. I faced my fears, stood up to the bullies, and I also won a lot of surprise support. There were a number of people in the audience who came to watch the open meeting. Some people came to support JD and they didn't know who I was yet. However, after the meeting, they ran up to me and told me that after they witnessed how JD and his allies treated me and their totally childish and petty behavior, they were so turned off by them and glad that I stood up to them that they ditched their support for him and came over to Team DeAnna. I actually won some of my best campaign volunteers that night. JD and his team thought they were winning by berating me and trying to tear me down in public, and in the end they may have won their petty little battle in their minds, but they definitely lost the war. The people who came over to my side afterwards and joined my campaign team said they were utterly horrified and humiliated by the behavior of JD and some of those group members, because God forbid if any new Republicans saw that charade and thought that the whole Republican party was like that — they would run far away!

I continued to share the truth about JD on my social media, too, and stopped holding back out of politeness. My campaign also produced and released a scathing compare-and-contrast ad about him, entitled *"4-Time Loser,"* which was awesome and people loved it. My digital warriors started flooding his tweets and livestreams with unsavory screenshots from him and bits of information. Meme artists made hilarious picture and video memes with JD's head on a rhino's body, and they quickly circulated the Internet. People took screenshots of his FEC reports sending money to the smear blogger Andrew Parks, and my supporters posted those every time he made disparaging comments about me online or tried to pass around those hit pieces.

The FOX news reporter Sara Carter even published an interview with both of us on her media site and kept tweeting it out. It was a side-by-side comparison with both of our pictures on the cover, and the title: "Two Republicans are running in California against Nancy Pelosi." *Yikes* — it was a bit nerve-wracking to see this article pitting us against each other in a competition for everyone to judge, especially given that Carter is such a high-profile journalist with millions of followers. It begged the reader to basically vote on one of us and pick a team. On his side, his headshot of course looked like the prototypical, polished, Establishment Republican; and for my side, rather than ask me for a professional headshot, the editors grabbed an old random picture of me dressed very casually, definitely not one I would have used! As usual, JD spent much of his interview talking crap about me and slandering me. I mostly just stuck to facts. In the end, every time she posted the article up on Twitter, which was about five different times in the weeks leading up to the election, the comment ratio was enormously in my favor! Thousands of people flooded the comments with support for me, saying they were on Team DeAnna and calling out JD for being a loser and a RINO, posting the pictures of his face on a rhino's body along with many other unsavory words about their experiences with him. It was great to see that people saw through the "perfect" veneer and could spot a true patriot with genuine intentions from an Establishment phony. It was glorious.

Going through this experience taught me that in the political world, everything and everyone are fair game, and nothing is off limits for what your opponents may attempt to do to win. It taught me that you have to see yourself as being not only on a level playing field as everyone else, but truly above their "rank." Meaning, my opponents were much older and more seasoned than I, as a young up-and-comer politician. I was raised to always respect elderly and authority, and keep a classy and gracious attitude toward them, regardless of how they may act. But in the political world, I learned that if I allowed their arrogance and years of experience to perceive myself on a lower level than them, then I was susceptible to bullying and intimidation. I had to retrain my brain to think of my opponents and those aiding them as my *enemies in war*, rather than "older and wiser authority figures" — and act and react accordingly. See, the older or more deeply entrenched political folks see themselves as *entitled* to their positions and they use their power to their advantage, knowing they'll eat a young newcomer alive if she or he doesn't project power and strength. In order to gain respect from others, you must send the message that you are a formidable opponent who is on the same level as them, or even on a *higher* level than them, and one who fights fire with fire — regardless of how old you are, how new to the game you are, and how deeply entrenched and seasoned they are.

CHAPTER 15

MASTER YOUR SOCIAL MEDIA GAME

"Timid men... prefer the calm of despotism to the boisterous sea of liberty."
— **Thomas Jefferson**

S ocial media is your BEST FRIEND when you are running a campaign or wanting to be a badass leader for your cause. You absolutely must use social media to the fullest. If you're not a "social media person," you're going to learn to become one... and fast. Social media is how people will hear your authentic voice. It's how people will get to know you and trust you. It's how you will be able to amplify your voice and message. It's how you'll position yourself as the badass leader in your race. It's how you'll gain support and a loyal following. All of these things will translate to more votes and a huge platform.

Social media is NOT solely going to translate into votes, however. Many people who will be voting in your district are not on social media, so you'd be a fool to rely strictly on your social media following for votes. However, it's the most powerful way for you to build your platform, get attention, earn media, and give yourself the most advantageous position to win the most votes.

The following is my blueprint for becoming a political rockstar on social media:

- **First, create a Twitter, Facebook, Periscope, Instagram, and YouTube account for your campaign.** If you already have those accounts, then you may want to consider changing your name (handle) to reflect your political campaign. Or at the very least, understand that you will be transitioning from personal posting to professional and political posting. Choose a name that will be "evergreen" — so it can remain accurate and current even after the campaign is over. Once you get your blue checkmark, you cannot change your handle. Since my name, DeAnna Lorraine already was taken (how dare they!), I chose the name @Deanna4Congress. The only issue now is that I realized later that I cannot change my name or else I will lose my "blue checkmark." So, I guess I am a congresswoman forever and ever, regardless of the election results!

- **Next, create your "public figure" Facebook page — which is different from a basic profile.** Once you get your Facebook page set up, start the process of getting approved to push paid ads through Facebook. When you run a campaign or even manage a company, you're going to want to run ads on Facebook. In order to run ads, you have to go through an approval process. The approval process can be arduous and lengthy, so you should create your Facebook page for your political campaign and start the ad approval process right away, even before you officially launch. Get that coveted blue checkmark on your Twitter, Instagram, and Facebook profiles.

- **Tweet and post daily — at least several times a day.** You should be tweeting very early in the morning, then throughout the day as breaking news and trending topics unfold. If you can't personally tweet and post, then have a social media manager or a campaign team member do it for you. You need to be posting at a bare minimum of three times every day on all your platforms (except Instagram, which requires less posting) in order to build and maintain your platform.

- **Take advantage of MEMEs!** Memes are a brilliant way to get your message across and be memorable. Video and picture memes make a lasting impression and are easy for people to share. I created them and used them on a regular basis during my campaign and still do! Special shout-out to the talented @SolMemes who created some incredibly badass memes for me.

- **Create memes for:**

  - Your best quotes, mic drop-worthy soundbites, and hashtags.

  - A funny or thought-provoking illustration of a trending news topic.

  - Your head on top of a superhero's body, or another character in a movie scene or "real life" scene that was savage.

  - Memes depicting your opponent(s).

- **Use a special hashtag and always take advantage of hashtags.** Choose and use hashtags throughout your campaign that will help brand you. I used: *#RINOSlayer, #DemDisruptor, #PelosiForPrison,* and *#NancyTearsDeAnnaCares* a lot through my campaign.

- **Build your tribe and engage with them regularly.** Find the followers of your favorite influencers and leaders. Click on their followers, and follow all of them. You want to follow as many people as possible who are like-minded, and you will keep growing. As long as you're posting consistently and following the rest of my blueprint here, you should have a high percentage of those follow you back.

- **Join Twitter and Facebook groups.** Join as many Twitter and Facebook groups of like-minded people as you possibly can. Share your tweets and posts in those groups and get to know the members. Share their posts as well so it's reciprocal.

- **Continue to draw stark contrasts between you and your opposition on your social media.** Whenever your opponent does or says something crazy, stupid, negligent, or just bad, be one of the first to comment on it and call them out.

- **Share what YOU would do differently, and your vision for America and/or your district.** Don't only attack your opponent, however. Too much attacking without any positivity or solutions starts sounding like you're too negative. Mix it up by proposing solutions, ideas, and sharing your vision. What would you do differently than your opponent? How would you improve things? What plan or solution can you propose? What is your vision? Share those things, too.

- **Get merchandise set up in the beginning.** Create merchandise for your campaign or cause. Get cool designs made of shirts, hats, mugs, bumper stickers, and other paraphernalia. Get those produced early, because they can take a few weeks to create and ship out. Then wear and promote your merchandise throughout your campaign. Give shirts and hats to all of your campaign team members and volunteers. Take photos with everyone wearing them. When people receive their shirt or other merchandise, encourage them to snap a picture or video of themselves wearing it and tag you in the photo on social media!

- **Make use of videos and video ads.** Videos and video ads are very powerful and persuasive! Take and produce a lot of videos throughout your campaign. Start with a dynamic, high-quality video announcing your campaign that highlights who you are, who you're running against, what you stand for, and your top goals for the district or country. Make a few more campaign ads throughout your run and get as many people as possible to share them.

- **Don't be intimidated. Don't listen to the haters.** Haters are gonna hate on social media. Don't feed the trolls. As soon as I made it on to "Right Wing Watch" and "Media Matters," trolls were hot on my trail watching all my content closely on social media. It's like they unleashed a never-ending army of trolls after me who, like leeches, suddenly latch on out of nowhere onto my tweets and start ridiculing me with the same, parroted talking points. It's annoying, but I usually just block them and go on with my day. I rarely argue with or debate people who leave nasty comments online — it will just drain your energy and make you seem petty or emotional. It's usually better to just ignore them and understand that the more popular you get, the more trolls there will be. Keep a good sense of humor and upbeat spirit for the majority of your social media posts.

- **Keep your eyes on the news, and be the first to comment and weigh in.** You want to be known as the go-to leader in your race, and the go-to expert on your opponent, in your district and state. The first thing I always do in the morning is check the news, Twitter, and Facebook for headlines on which I could weigh-in. Then I try to be one of the first to write a tweet and often a short video with my comments and thoughts on the topic.

- **Live stream and use Periscope regularly.** People want to see you in action. They want to see you talk and engage. They begin to establish trust and confidence in you when you speak to them. So, I created a live Periscope and Facebook video at least a few times a week, if not every day, then at the same time each day, so people start looking forward to your live streams and you train them to watch.

For those of you who have any introversion or social anxiety, you'll need to train yourself and develop those social skills while running your campaign. You can do this!

At the time this book went to print, I had hundreds of thousands of followers on my social media outlets — and the numbers continue to grow. I remain front and center of conversations, the latest news, and hot topics. People gravitate to me for my style of honesty, humor, and optimism. Soon if you follow my strategies, you will have a great following and platform too!

Get the President's Attention

There's no way to guarantee that you'll get retweeted by the president of the United States, but it's always worth a try! If your tweets are well written with solid information, especially relevant to a trending topic of the day, then it's possible that the president will see them and retweet. It also helps to post quality replies under his tweets as he has a higher chance of seeing them that way — and you'll be seen by other people, too. I've been retweeted a bunch of times by him now. Also, try to get retweeted by other high-profile celebrities and political influencers, because any retweets by well-known public figures will also boost your profile.

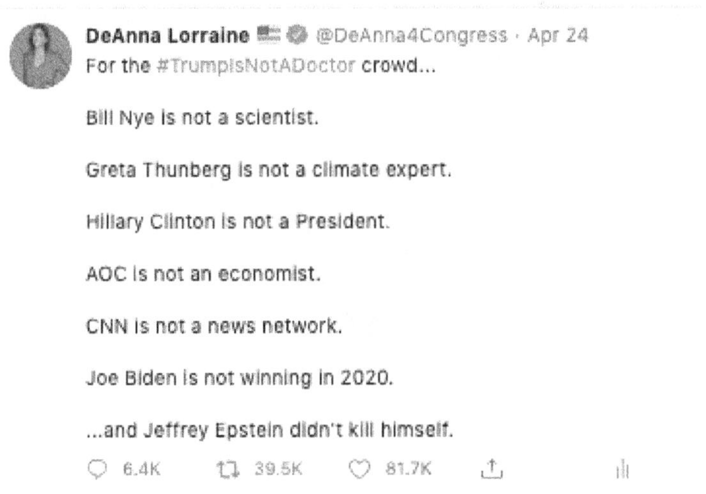
DeAnna Lorraine @DeAnna4Congress · Apr 24
For the #TrumpIsNotADoctor crowd...
Bill Nye is not a scientist.
Greta Thunberg is not a climate expert.
Hillary Clinton is not a President.
AOC is not an economist.
CNN is not a news network.
Joe Biden is not winning in 2020.
...and Jeffrey Epstein didn't kill himself.
6.4K
39.5K
81.7K

Another one of my tweets that went viral and retweeted by the president.

I was so excited the first time I found out the president had retweeted my tweet. I was sitting in my apartment with my campaign managers, strategizing for an upcoming event. All of a sudden my phone started buzzing: "Omg, did the president just retweet you?" I looked at my phone and sure enough, the president retweeted me. We all started screaming and jumping up and down. Every time he retweets me it's an exciting day!

**Make sure that you're a part of my growing community of fearless patriots as we fight together in the war of our lives to take back America. Join my Inner Circle email list and Telegram group —this is our "safe space" to freely communicate about all of these issues, organize, mobile rallies and other important actions that we need to take to fight back & take back America: DeannaLorraine.com/inner-circle.

*Also be sure you subscribe to my Podcast, **Taking Back America!** I broadcast every Tuesday, Wednesday & Thursday from **YouTube, Periscope, iTunes,** and other channels and I keep you updated on the latest breaking news as well as my upcoming events.*

YouTube.com/c/DeAnnaLorraine

Twitter.com/DeAnna4Congress

CHAPTER 16

WELL-BEHAVED WOMEN NEVER MAKE HISTORY

"No great mind has ever existed without a touch of madness."
— Aristotle

★ ★ ★

You can tow the line, play by all the rules, and play it "safe" in life, in your professional life — and in the political world. The benefit of doing that is you will be, well, "safe" and you won't make any waves with people. Or, you can be your own person, color outside the lines a bit, and break some rules. You can be a bold, badass warrior and *misbehave* sometimes. That's who I've been in my life, and it's how I've chosen to be with my campaign and political career — and it's made an impact. There is so much truth to this expression: *"Well-behaved Women Never Make History."*

Look at Rosa Parks. Look at Phyllis Schlafly. Look at Amelia Earhart. What do they all have in common? They made history not by towing the line and "not making any waves" — they *intentionally* made waves to shake people up and make an impact!

My grandmother is the same way and I have to say, I inherited her rebellious streak. One of my favorite things she did was how she changed the rules of a certain gender game by fighting the status quo. Back in the 1950s, while married to my grandfather, he was at work for the day and she wanted to buy a new lawnmower, because theirs broke. She went to the hardware store and took it to the counter, only for the manager to refuse to sell it to her. "I'm sorry ma'am, we don't sell heavy operating machinery to women, for safety purposes. Whenever your husband comes home he can come back and buy it then," the store manager said. "Are you serious?" my grandmother complained. "I grew up on a farm in New Mexico, with seven brothers and I was raised doing everything required to manage the farm, from shooting and skinning turkeys to mowing the grass, operating the tractors, and everything in between. I know how to get my hands dirty and handle heavy machinery!" But, they still denied her and insisted that they only sold that type of equipment to men.

So, she drove home and angrily blew up the telephone lines of the most popular radio station until someone answered. She shared her story on live radio and complained how silly and sexist it was that she was refused service just because she was a woman. She got the radio hosts talking about it, and lots of other angry women and men calling in with their support. Well, her protests were successful and lo and behold, the store ended up changing their long-standing rules in order to sell all products to women — just because of my grandmother! So, don't be afraid to make some noise and raise some hell. I certainly am not!

Making it Rain Liberal Tears with My Pelosi for Prison Campaign

As Nancy Pelosi's ridiculous sham impeachment hearings were heating up, I became more and more infuriated at her actions and with her fanning the flames of an already divided country. I was getting messages from all over the nation with Americans equally angry at Pelosi. It was building up inside me, and I felt like I had to do something BIG and bold to send a strong message and put her in her place. I wanted to be a voice for all who felt they were spit in the face by Nancy and didn't have any platform to express their anger. I also needed to deploy more strategies to bring local name recognition to my campaign. Since JD had the upper hand as chairman of the local GOP and had run for office many times in the district, I had to assume that many people didn't know my name yet, whereas they probably knew his. What could I do to call Nancy out and at the same time bring local name recognition and visibility for my campaign?

A lightbulb suddenly went off: how about I do one of those big spotlights in the sky? Or a petition or TV ad? Well, I researched the spotlight idea, but found out you could only project a logo via spotlight into the sky, and I wanted a full message, not just my campaign logo. Hmmm, how about flying a plane with a provocative message? I was so tired of seeing her scapegoat and point the finger at President Trump, when it was all just a big projection to cover up her own wrongdoings and crimes against Americans.

I know. How about... *"Pelosi for Prison!"* It immediately felt right. It got the point across, it conveyed the thoughts of many, and it also was catchy enough to make a hashtag out of it. As I asked around, lots of people immediately loved the idea. However, some warned against it and told me absolutely to not do it — they said it was too divisive and provocative for San Francisco and it would get only negative attention. I went back and forth on it, mulling it over for a week. My idea was to have the "Pelosi for Prison" on one side, and then have "Pelosi for Prison — Vote for DeAnna" on the other side in Mandarin, since there is such a large demographic of Chinese voters in San Francisco and I wanted to make them feel included as well.

Then Nancy did something so horrific that it was the perfect precursor to what I was about to do. She ripped up the president's *State of the Union* speech, behind his back, in front of the world. News pundits were stunned and speechless on live TV. The comments flooded in and social media went wild with memes and replays. The stage was set and it was perfect. At that moment I was so glad I stuck with my guns and got the banner created. Her disgraceful action was like a gift handed to my campaign.

I decided to create a petition that went along with the banner called "Pelosi for Prison." The petition along with the corresponding website I set up for it would prompt people to sign the petition if they would like to see Nancy Pelosi investigated for *her* "crimes against America," particularly her egregious act of disrespect ripping up the president's State of the Union speech behind his back for the whole world to see. What else could we promote along with this? How about T-shirts?! With the help of a designer, we also created awesome Pelosi for Prison T-shirts that we offered for sale on the second page of the petition.

Since I was running in very lefty San Francisco, I unfortunately had the experience a few times where I contacted a company to get a campaign item made, like brochures, shirts, or buttons printed, and once I started giving them the details that I was running against Nancy Pelosi and that I was a Republican, they shrieked and turned me away. It actually happened quite frequently where I would go to a restaurant or a bar and the waiter would be super friendly, then suddenly would turn cold and nasty toward me. It took me a little while to figure it out, but I soon connected the dots that once they saw my credit card that read "DeAnna for Congress" on it, they Googled me and stopped being friendly to me. Oh well, I was used to it by then.

The second phone call I made to a banner flying company was like another gift. Once the manager asked me what exactly I wanted printed on the huge banner, I hesitated for a minute, said a little prayer, and was already expecting him to hang the phone up on me afterwards. "Well... it's a political banner... It's going to say (holding my breath) "Pelosi for Prison." (Pause) He said, "Pelosi for Prison? Are you running a campaign against her or something?" I said, "Yes... " Then, he said, "Are you a Republican or Democrat?" Me cautiously, "Republican..." (Pause). He shouted excitedly, "Woah, that's awesome!" "Wow, really?" I responded. He confirmed, "Oh my gosh I can't STAND Pelosi! Get that nasty hag out of there!" I was so relieved. What are the odds he was a huge Conservative and it turned out his company was also the one who was hired to create and fly the "Hillary for Prison" banners, from the Alex Jones InfoWars campaign. He said he was incredibly excited to work with me and would give me a great deal on everything. It's the little wins like those that are exciting and confirm that you're on the right track!

We went back and forth with the design and messaging for the banner, because it needed to look just right. Unfortunately the banner could only be one-sided, and when he tried to fit the Chinese characters on the one side it was just too busy and difficult to read. At last, after much refining, the banner looked perfect.

I coordinated a group of my campaign volunteers to come out for the official "launch party" for the flyover banner. We also felt like it was wise to hire security guards to escort and surround us. I had no idea what the response would be like, but given the track record of Antifa in San Francisco, I was fully expecting the plane to incite riots or have molotov cocktails thrown at us! We were able to get a group of Bikers for Trump to come out and be with us to protect from any shenanigans that Antifa or any crazed leftists may cause.

It took a lot of coordination of many different moving parts, but finally we were ready for the big day. We all waited at the edge of The Embarcadero, wearing my red DeAnna for Congress shirts and facing the Bay Bridge waiting for the plane to come. I was able to text back and forth with the pilot, so we could coordinate exactly where and when he should be flying around during the several hours he'd be flying the banner, which was pretty cool.

I chose the Embarcadero area, because: a) It was an ideal place to see it and take pictures of it, since the plane could get low to the ground; and, b) That is the area where Kate Steinle got shot and killed by an illegal immigrant, and I wanted to raise attention to that as yet another "Crime Against Americans" that Nancy Pelosi committed. She continuously prioritizes the lives of illegal immigrants over Americans and neglects the safety and well-being of American citizens over and over. Enough is enough.

The Pilot texted saying he was running a little behind due to "mechanical errors" on the plane and fog. Darn! I was getting so anxious, because I wanted everything to go perfectly. We waited... and waited. Finally, there he was, approaching from the Bay Bridge coming from Hayward Airport. "There it is!" I yelled. Everyone looked up and got so excited. Then once they read the full message, "Pelosi for Prison," everyone started jumping and screaming. Seeing the plane pull a huge 80-foot by 25-foot banner with Pelosi for Prison and my DeAnna for Congress logo flying over the most Liberal city in America and Nancy Pelosi's backyard... It was epic! I knew then that I had made the right decision and I was so glad I followed my instincts.

The banner proceeded to fly over the Financial District area, shocking San Francisco workers and drivers as they looked up. He flew it slowly over the Marina area, the parks, and golf courses. It flew over City Hall, raining Liberal tears. Some people looked up and laughed when they saw what it said and actually said, "Right on!" Other people yelled obscenities and probably would have shot it down if they had a gun on them. One angry leftist guy posted on social media that he saw it fly right past his office window during a meeting and it "rudely interrupted" the meeting. LOL, sorry!

As we started uploading videos and pictures of the plane and banner onto social media, it got picked up by media outlets quickly and went viral, then making it into a bunch of news stories. If you Google "Pelosi for Prison" you can read some of them. The campaign definitely accomplished my goals and was a bold risk that paid off. I got thousands of signatures of people signing the *Pelosi for Prison* petition, about $10,000 in donations, and the T-shirts were selling like hotcakes. People started using the video clips of the flying banner as memes and posted them underneath Pelosi's tweets.

It brought a lot of attention to my campaign and name recognition, both locally and nationally. A now famous hashtag sprung out of it along with memes that people still use today, and it certainly got people talking!

I'm so glad I didn't listen to the naysayers telling me it was too risky of a move. At least 99 percent of the messages and feedback I got were positive. People everywhere who were outraged by Pelosi felt like their feelings were expressed by the swift "disciplinary action" I took. Just as I felt, scolding her verbally on social media wasn't enough — she had to be called out in a much bigger way.

WJ THE WESTERN JOURNAL

News

NEWS

'Pelosi for Prison': GOP Challenger Takes Flight Against Pelosi After Speaker's Recent Antics

DeAnna Lorraine launched an aerial campaign over San Francisco on Feb. 6 to call attention to what she believes are crimes against the American people . . (Courtesy of DeAnna Lorraine)

One of the many articles published about my Pelosi for Prison flyover banner campaign.

After getting such a positive response, I flew the banner again a few weeks later. This time I gave everyone a head's up of when and where in the city it would fly and I texted updates throughout the day of where specifically the banner was about to head next, so locals could come out and see it themselves. I sat at a restaurant on the pier for a quick bite and two of the restaurant managers were talking about it. It turned out they were silent Trump supporters. I told them I was the person behind the banner, which earned me more voters!

I REALLY wanted to fly it one more time during my campaign, either at the big CPAC convention in Washington, DC or at the Daytona 500 races in Florida. It would have been perfect! Unfortunately we found out that there is a 30-mile radius of protected airspace around Washington, DC and the president, so it could not be flown at those events, which was a huge bummer. But, I still have the banner and a lot of requests regularly from people wanting me to fly it again, so I intend on flying it a few more times before the general election.

Shaking Up the City with My Mobile Billboards

"It's hard to lead a cavalry charge if you think you look funny on a horse."
— **Adlai E. Stevenson**

What other ways could I increase local name recognition? After brainstorming more ideas, I thought of driving around town with a huge mobile billboard truck. It seemed like another great way to cause a stir and also have my name displayed around the city. I knew my opponents were probably not brave enough to think of nor execute something like that. Boom! That was it. I looked around and found a mobile billboard company to work with and got it set up.

I again coordinated a group of my campaign volunteers to gather around for the mobile billboard's grand debut. It was a very cool experience! Imagine a huge truck with big LED screens on all three sides displaying any combination of videos, images, words, and music with any element swapped out at any time. I decided to have one side of the truck flash images, videos, and words of Nancy Pelosi's "failures" — images of homelessness with homeless veterans on the streets, people shooting up drugs, needles, trash, and feces on the streets, poverty and destruction. I also displayed the video clips of her ripping up the State of the Union, and chomping on her dentures. Then on the other side I had images and videos of optimism, hope, and patriotism. Highlights of me and my campaign, media clips, President Trump's rallies, American flags waving, and stats about job growth and a booming economy. On the back and lower-third of the truck was my website, a call to action to vote for DeAnna Lorraine against Nancy Pelosi for Congress in the March 3rd election.

And again, there were naysayers who cautioned me against the idea: "But... no one does that in San Francisco... I've never seen anyone drive a mobile billboard truck around." "But... won't you be scared, driving that billboard truck around in the most Liberal city?" Once again, I ignored them and went with my gut.

All of my campaign volunteers cheered when the billboard truck arrived, and people walking by stopped to look at the images, stunned and confused, as they had never seen anything like it in San Francisco. The truck only had seats for two, so I grabbed one of my volunteers, hopped in the truck, and off we went. At first it was a little scary driving slowly down the busy streets of San Francisco, because it was so brazen, but it definitely captured eyeballs — everyone stopped and looked at the truck. Once they saw the display, many were outraged and triggered.

Me in front of my dynamic mobile billboard in San Francisco.

Then the fun REALLY began when we started blasting the "Proud to be an American" song down the streets of the Financial District and The Embarcadero. Jaws dropped to the floor and people were taking pictures and videos, yelling at us, flipping us off, and going nuts, like demons in need of an exorcism. However, we also saw a lot of silent Conservatives, tipping their hats to us, giving us thumbs up, and waving. One construction worker even pulled out a MAGA hat from his back pocket and yelled, "Thank you! We need more of you here!"

Believe it or not, the most receptive area we rolled into was actually Chinatown. The first time we rolled into the neighborhood slowly with "Proud to be an American" blasting, everyone on the streets looked up and started cheering and waving! Then when we stopped and parked the truck, I would jump out and shake hands with them while they took pictures and videos with me. It turned out that many in the Chinese community love Trump, and I earned myself many new voters. We ended up spending a lot of the time driving the billboard around the Chinatown area, because the reception was so warm and everyone got so excited when we drove through.

We also spent a lot of time driving slowly through the farmer's market. That was a LOT of fun, because once we started blasting "Proud to be an American" everyone's heads turned up and looked at the billboard with me in the front seat waving. We got some applause, and many boos, as well. One time we had a mob of people break out into chants screaming at us *"Hey Hey! Ho Ho! Racist Trump has got to go! Hey Hey! Ho Ho! Racist Trump has got to go!"* I thought they might try to actually tip the truck over! Watching Liberals' heads explode from a simple song and a billboard definitely was a blast, not going to lie.

I even held a meme contest on Twitter, where I asked people to send in all of their best memes of Pelosi and I used my favorite ones on the billboard.

We ended up having the billboard truck drive around for four consecutive days. By the end of the four days, word had spread about the billboard truck around town and as it drove by, I had local supporters shouting, "I love you, DeAnna!" Many of them stopped what they were doing to come meet me and shake my hand. Then due to popular demand, we even brought it back for the four days leading up to the election, reminding people to vote for me.

My mobile billboard cruising through the city!

Ellen Zhou is a former Republican mayoral candidate in San Francisco and a friend of mine.. She ran against incumbent Democrat London Breed, who had a well-oiled machine of fundraising and media working for her, while Zhou was the underdog and subsequently had a harder time building local name recognition and publicity. Well, she found a brilliant way to get around that issue and made a huge splash, both locally and nationally — and she did it by bucking the rules and misbehaving. Three weeks before her election, she had a billboard installed overnight in a busy area of San Francisco. It was a very controversial and provocative billboard, which depicted the current mayor and her opponent, London Breed, lounging at her office desk with her feet up in the air with her high heels kicked off, in a racy red dress, smoking a cigar while holding stacks of cash. On the other side of the billboard was a picture of a man carrying a young girl with the quotes under it: "Stop slavery and human trafficking in SF," and "Vote Ellen Zhou Nov 5th for Mayor." By noon on the very day that her billboard was installed, the news had erupted in a firestorm of articles and TV coverage. Thousands of people were talking about it on social media, some with outrage, and others who saw her as a badass for having the guts to put up such a bold and honest billboard. Zhou was slammed by many publicly as being "racist" and "sexist," and it even sparked a group of elected San Francisco leaders to hold a press conference and protest against it, demanding it be taken down, because it was so "offensive." But despite all the pressure and outrage, Zhou stuck to her guns and never apologized to the haters or backpedaled. Whether people loved it or hated it, this candidate took a risk that, I believe, paid off. It brought her a huge wave of local and national media attention during the ever-important weeks leading up to her election, more people became familiar with her name and face, and ignited her fanbase to be even more motivated to vote for her.

It can be hard sometimes to follow your instincts, stand up for your beliefs, or go against the grain. When you misbehave or do something that's bold, it can be scary and difficult to stay strong. You may second guess yourself, think you're crazy, and feel tempted to give in to people pressuring or shaming you. It doesn't necessarily feel good to feel like you're not "in the club," and an outsider. You may wonder when the majority of people are thinking and saying one thing, and encouraging you to do the same, but you simply feel something in your heart that is different from the crowd. If you feel a certain way or believe strongly about something, stand strong in that truth, follow your instincts and you will be rewarded in the end for doing so. Remember, the people who have made the biggest difference in the world and made major marks in history weren't "normal" people who always colored inside the lines and whose thoughts were in lockstep with everyone else. They were individuals who colored outside the lines, broke the rules, and misbehaved. To quote

Aristotle, "No great mind has ever existed without a touch of madness."

CHAPTER 17

HOW TO MASTER YOUR
*FU*NDRAISING GAME

"Is life so dear, or peaceful so sweet, as to be purchased at the price of chains and slavery? Forbid it, Almighty God! I know not what course others may take, but as for me, give me liberty or give me death!"
— **Patrick Henry**

F undraising is obviously an essential component to every campaign or cause, but it's often the hardest part for many people. The truth is you simply cannot get your campaign to truly gain significant momentum, as well as be successful, if you don't generate mucho moolah. You really don't want to have to dip into any of your own savings either. Campaigns require much more money than many people think, and the number one reason why people end up quitting their campaign is lack of funds. However, my theory is that fundraising doesn't have to be stressful and daunting, nor feel like "work." Over time during my campaign, I learned to reframe the association in my mind and come up with creative ways to turn the act of fundraising into *"fun*draising."

I didn't necessarily raise a ridiculous amount of money, and I started fundraising the latest out of all my opponents. However, in just six months, I raised more than $260,000 — which was not TOO shabby for the shorter runway I had. My fundraising had gained so much momentum at the point of the primary election, that if I had those few more months to fundraise, and it hadn't been cut short due to the election getting moved up this year, I'm confident I could have raised at least half a million. It took a little while for the funds to really start flowing though, so you should start fundraising before even publicly announcing your campaign.

Fundraising Game Plan

Phone Fundraising Tips:

- **One of the first items you will want to spend money on is your district's up-to-date voter data.** This will give you the most accurate data of your registered voters in your district, their contact information, and voter history. This is crucial information, as you will need it to determine what your overall "universe" looks like to court voters, your campaign promotional material mailing list, and your fundraising target list.

- **Create a spreadsheet of your personal contacts.** List all of your friends, family members, then colleagues and other acquaintances. Mark the contacts who you feel confident are the most likely to donate to your effort. Block off two hours every day and start calling away. Start with the marked names first, then go down the list with the others. It was hard for me at first, but with time I got in the groove. Keep conversations relatively short and to the point, no more than five to 10 minutes. Sound excited and confident from the get-go, this IS exciting! You have decided to run for office! You have the courage to put yourself out there in a big way, because you're so committed to making a positive difference in America and you need their help to get there.

- **Be bold with your requests.** Don't ask for the lowest possible number, like $25 or $100. Ask for the highest number first, then go down from there. Remember, these are grown adults. Asking for $1,000 may seem like a lot to you, but it's not a lot for many people that you'll ask. Remember this — it's not your job to determine how much or how little they can afford anyway — often people will surprise you! There were times I would assume how much someone could afford based on their occupation and then they surprised me.

Email Fundraising:

- **Create an email fundraising machine.** Partner with someone or a group who can manage the email fundraising aspect for you. Someone with experience, as well as a strong track record for raising lots of campaign money. This individual or company would set up your email fundraising platform, create the copy for your fundraising emails, and provide you with the targeted donor list.

- **Share or rent email contact lists.** If you have the funds, consider hiring someone to do this for you, if not, it is something you can do yourself and save precious campaign dollars. There are many companies, clubs, individuals, and organizations with huge, largely Republican email lists, and they may consider renting out their list to others. Whatever email list you rent or share would still usually require you to give a percentage of the funds raised to them, however.

Events and in-person fundraising:

Much of your fundraising will be in person. Anytime you are out and about or at events, there's an opportunity for you to raise funds. Whenever you are speaking at or attending an event, always carry literature with you, such as business cards, campaign materials, as well as credit card slips and envelopes with your campaign logos on them. Whenever you speak at an event, be sure to put a packet with your campaign literature along with the credit card slips and envelopes at every seat. At the end of your talk, ASK them for their donation.

Whenever you talk to anyone about your campaign, get in the habit of asking them if they are able to donate to your campaign before leaving the conversation.

Social media fundraising:

If you follow the strategies in this book then your social media following should be growing *bigly*. So, use your social media profiles as outlets to fundraise as well.

I included my fundraising link, along with a great campaign video, pinned to all my social media profiles. I reminded people to donate to my campaign every few days.

As I mentioned above, I always let them know whenever an FEC deadline was approaching, my fundraising goal, and how much I still needed.

Consider hosting creative fundraising contests and "fundraising-a-thons."

- Anyone donating $100 or more in a 24-hour period, would receive a personal thank you tweet and I would follow them on social media. That encouraged a lot of people to donate $100 or more! Everyone likes a personal shout-out and thank you. Sometimes I would live-stream for hours, chatting, doing live Q&As, hanging out, and encouraging them to donate. When they donated I would do a big shout-out to them and often would personally call them.

- Offer supporters campaign merchandise if they donate a specific amount in a given time period, like a campaign mug, T-shirt, buttons, etc. People want to help, especially if you make it fun and engaging, and they also love to see the number for your goal amount climbing up.

- Have fun with your social media following! Remember that often people want to help you if they like you, they just need to be reminded frequently that your campaign needs funds in order to be victorious.

Media fundraising:

During each media appearance or interview, direct the audience to your website and ask them to donate to your campaign, at least once or twice during the interview. Be sure to spell out your web address as well.

Other tactics to make you a badass fundraiser:

- **Communicate every quarterly FEC fundraising deadline to all of your followers/supporters through every source you use:** social media, email blasts, rented lists, etc. Include the FEC closing date, your fundraising goal for that period, and how much more you need to hit your goal.

- **Let people know specifically *how* you'll be spending the funds at that time.** People like to know how their hard-earned money will be used and there may be something specific you'll be doing that will get them excited to support. For example: *"I need $5,000 more, so that I can get my yard signs made, my buttons, shirts, and the first round of video ads produced."*

- **The answer always will be no if you don't ask.** The answer will most likely be *no* if you are very hesitant. The answer will more likely be *yes* if you ask confidently and excitedly, almost assuming the sale. Treat every person like they are powerful, wealthy, and eager to help, not weak, poor, and like you're "bothering them." And remember *YOU* are powerful. *You* can do this!

- **Remember this:** *When* you actually get elected into office, *because* you're such a political badass, you'll have to do a lot more of asking and negotiating for things — and much *bigger* things and larger quantities of moolah — so you must start building that "asking and negotiating" muscle, now!

- **Create fundraising contests with friends who also are campaigning.** I'm a believer in friendly competition, because it motivates me. So, while I was running I created contests with friends who also were running for Congress. It was fun and sometimes lit a fire under me to go the extra mile.

- **Celebrate milestones!** I remember when I first broke the $100,000 mark. For a while I was wondering if I ever would break it. But I just kept at it, kept praying, continued fundraising live streams, and then one great day, we saw the Revv account go from $99,000 to $100,000. We were so excited! It's definitely a milestone when you break through the $100,000 mark, and every fundraising milestone achieved should be acknowledged and celebrated. It boosted my confidence and made the next $100,000 much easier, because I knew I was capable of it.

I raised a lot of money with my "Pelosi for Prison" petition. Remember that after folks signed the petition, there was an option to purchase *Pelosi for Prison* T-shirts, in addition to a fundraising button. I raised about $10,000 just from that campaign alone.

Remember:

Communicate exactly how their money will be used, share your goals, how much you need, and within what timeframe. Make your supporters and followers a part of your journey. People like to know how their money will be used. Don't give a lofty or vague goal — be specific.

- What creative things can you think of to motivate people to give to you?
- What incentives can you give them?
- What fun games can you play?
- The world is your playground. Think outside the box, brainstorm ideas, and you'll be amazed how fundraising truly can become *FUN*draising!

CHAPTER 18

KEEP A WINNING ATTITUDE AND YOUR FIRE LIT

"Attitude is a choice. Happiness is a choice. Optimism is a choice. Kindness is a choice. Giving is a choice. Respect is a choice. Whatever choice you make makes you. Choose wisely."
— **Roy T. Bennett, *The Light in the Heart***

There will be times during your campaign when you're going to have to reignite your fire. There will be mornings where you'll wake up and think *whyyyyy did I do this?!* That's okay and normal, but recognize when that fire inside you is getting dimmed, or its been stamped out altogether due to fatigue or attacks against you. And reignite your fire.

There will be lots of stimuli flying in your face, and lots of people — especially your opponents — who will attempt to distract you to kill your fire and momentum. Don't get distracted. Don't feel defeated. Be like a race horse with horse blinders. It's called a "race" for a reason! You cannot be lazy or self-pitying in this game. Keep your eyes on the prize when the going gets tough.

KEEP A WINNING ATTITUDE AND YOUR FIRE LIT

You cannot act like a victim and spend days licking your wounds when you're getting knocked down. You cannot let haters get you down or allow yourself to feel defeated. Stay in the game and recreate your commitment and mindset of winning. Even if it looks on paper like the numbers aren't in your favor, believe you *can* and *will* win. Anything can happen to turn things around and change those numbers. The Universal Law of Attraction is very real, and if you start giving in to negative thoughts and you let your thoughts, your results, or others' negative words or attacks make you feel defeated and hopeless, you will start attracting more and more negative results, and you will seal a negative fate.

Winning Encompasses Both Actions and Mindset

You must maintain a mindset of certainty and faith. Always think of yourself as a winner, talk to yourself and others like you're a winner, and relate to yourself as a winner. Think, act, and talk like you've already won and see the world this way. Every day you should spend time, at least every morning and evening, visualizing your victory night. Visualize you winning and seeing those numbers on TV. Visualize you in office, walking around DC with swagger and making a massive impact in America with the causes you're championing. Remember your "Big Why" and your vision for the future of America for which you're fighting. And, most importantly, remember that America needs *you*. America needs *your voice and your leadership.*

Every day is a new day to turn the ride in your favor and execute actions that will increase your votes and visibility. This also is why it's so important that you have a strong support team who can bolster your confidence, remind you how awesome you are, and renew your spirit on days when you feel your spirit is falling. I'll remind you right now. You are AWESOME and brilliant!

Stay POSITIVE and communicate *strength,* leadership, positivity, and vision for the future. Remember, you can DO this! Don't lose heart. You are capable of winning. If you feel like you're having a bad or frustrating day, just dust yourself off, and pray. You're obviously an amazing and courageous human being, which is why you threw yourself in the fire to begin with and vowed to serve your country. You're a badass, a fighter, and light years ahead of most of the population who are just sitting on their butts complaining about stuff or trolling from their computers, yet not having the guts to do anything about it. God put this intention into your heart, now it's up to you to make it happen. Lean on your trusted advisors and loyal supporters. Learn from my crazy mistakes, so you don't have to learn the hard way. Review your accomplishments. Throw on a sexy fabulous power suit and look at your amazing self in the mirror. Say these words out loud: "You are more than enough. You have everything it takes to win and serve your country. You are going to make an important, powerful impact in America when you get elected."

You came this far. If I can get through this, you can, too! It's time to change out the corrupt Old Guard. You have done what most people are too afraid or unwilling to do. Now, finish the race! We are at war in America, and we need *you* and your unique voice in the fight! If you need someone to slap you and light a fire under you, feel free to holler at me.

YOU are talented and special. YOU are fully capable of doing this. You're a WINNER!

CHAPTER 19

HOW TO MASTER YOUR VOTER OUTREACH GAME

"The only thing that can stop this corrupt machine is you. *The only force strong enough to save our country is* us. *The only people brave enough to vote out this corrupt establishment is* you, *the American people."*
— **Donald J. Trump**

I f you're running for office, your ultimate goal is to *win*. In order to win, you obviously need to get the most votes. In the end, I did not win my primary election. Sadly! The candidate who got the most votes is... unfortunately, the radical Socialist, Shahid Buttar. So now, the only choice for my race of California-12 going into the general election is Nancy Pelosi... or the radical, Bernie Sanders-endorsed Socialist. Of course I was very disappointed, especially after how hard I worked, but there are many more things I learned that I'll share with you from which you definitely can learn and can help *you* increase your votes and WIN.

Getting out the vote (GOTV) is a comprehensive process which involves multiple facets, all working together. One of the first items you should do is to secure the voter data for your district. You need to understand your whole "universe" with whom you'll be interacting.

Set up your GOTV infrastructure:

- ❏ Voter data
- ❏ Texting platform
- ❏ Email platform
- ❏ ROBO calls and voicemail drops platform
- ❏ Flyers, window-signs, door-hangers, signs
- ❏ Door-knocking: voter precinct maps
- ❏ Events, engaging with voters, rallies
- ❏ Radio ads
- ❏ Town Hall and/or virtual Town Hall setup

Physical Presence

Step One: gathering your signatures.

In order to even make it onto the ballot, most districts and races require you to gather a certain number of signatures. For a congressional race in California, I needed between 40 to 60 verified signatures. The names for the signatures must match exactly with the individual's current registered voting address, otherwise they would be thrown out.

Find out early on in your campaign when your deadline is to turn in your signatures, and how many you need to qualify. I ended up getting 87 signatures in total, but it wasn't easy!

Get Your Signatures EARLY! Don't Wait till the Last Week!

During my campaign, I pretty much waited till the last two weeks to start gathering signatures. It was pouring rain and freezing nearly every day I went out, but I pounded the pavement and tried to hit at least 20 doors every day — after which I would reward myself by pigging out on San Francisco's finest cheap dim sum. The door knocking was tough though, because San Francisco is probably the least friendly and conducive place for campaigning and knocking on doors. Many, many voters live in apartments, so unless you know the gate code to get into the building or someone happens to be walking into or out of it while you approach, you're not getting in. And voters who live in homes almost always have a gated area where the doorbell is, for "homeless people prevention," so it takes a person a long time to get from inside their home to open their front gate, and it often seemed like a hassle for them. The best luck I had though was setting up camp at the weekend farmer's markets. Between 9 am to 1 pm there were thousands of people coming through the farmer's markets, so I was able to get dozens of signatures in short bursts of time. Even though I was dreading the signature-gathering process initially, it turned out to be a really beautiful and eye-opening experience in my campaign that I'll never forget.

Some highlights:

What I really enjoyed was that for the most part, at least in my experience and district, when I told people I was running for Congress and I needed their signature to qualify, they were happy to oblige. A lot of women thought it was so cool that a woman was running for office that they were okay with signing, even when they found out I was a Republican and they were a Democrat.

There was one older woman, though, who I won't forget. It was pouring rain outside and I got her signature. Yes! Her signature made my goal for the day and I couldn't wait to get out of the freezing cold and into a warm restaurant. After I packed up my things and started walking away, five minutes later she hunted me down and shouted, "Wait! Wait! I just realized I forgot to ask you, what party are you running as and do you support the president?" I could tell by her face she probably wasn't going to like the answer, but I said hurriedly "Republican... and I support Trump." Her face immediately turned to outrage and disgust, "Oh my God! You support the orange Hitler?! You are a Nazi, can I take my signature back? I didn't know you were a Trump-lover!" I have to admit I was freezing cold and really didn't want to have to give up that signature, so I perhaps selfishly said, "I'm so sorry ma'am! Your signature doesn't mean I'm going to Congress it just means I get to qualify and no I can't take signatures back unfortunately, sorrrry!" as I ran-walked away into the crowd away from her.

Then there was the time my Asian volunteers thought it would be a great idea to go to the Chinese Mennonite Church and get signatures from the Chinese church-goers there. We waited inside the church entrance and once the service finished, three of us stood with clipboards trying to get as many of them as possible to sign. Most of them ended up not being able to speak English, so they thought I was trying to sell them something or couldn't understand what the heck I was doing so there was a lot of confusion and raucous, with some downright angry. It wasn't quite as successful as we had hoped, but at least we tried!

Then there was the sweet blind man. After walking up a long flight of stairs, one doorbell I rang had several very loud and aggressive sounding dogs barking. Finally a man came to the door. "Hi, I'm looking to talk to Mr. and Mrs. Thompson?" "Well, I'm Mr. Thompson, but I don't have a Mrs..." "Oh, I'm sorry, it says here on the voter rolls that there is a Mrs. for some reason," I said. "Nope, it's just me and my dogs." "Well I'm running for Congress and I'd love to have your signature, so I can get on the ballot for the election."

We ended up having a long and lovely conversation. It turned out that he was a sweet blind man in his thirties and a strong Republican. He loved President Trump, because he said he hated how Liberals treat everyone like they're helpless and stupid, depending on the government to get by. He said as a blind man he's had to learn how to be self-sufficient his whole life and believes Americans are much more powerful when they learn to pull themselves up from their bootstraps, take personal responsibility for their lives, and have maximum personal liberty. It was really cool to hear that from someone who easily could be in a position to depend on other people, as well as the government.

We sat on his doorstep talking for a while and he admitted to me how much he wanted to have a "Mrs." Johnson. "I can't wait to vote for you in March, you definitely have my vote Ms. Lorraine!" he said. "And, if you have any time left over, can you also try to find me a wife? A nice patriotic woman like you?" He asked. I laughed and told him I would certainly keep an eye out for him and do my best! (Any takers out there for this catch?) It was these conversations with real voters, hearing about their lives and their concerns that really touched my heart and made it all worth it for me.

There was another memorable time where I knocked on the door, rang the doorbell a few times, and after starting to walk away the door finally slowly opened. An older guy opens his door with a huge cloud of weed smoke surrounding him and Tom Petty playing in the background. After talking to him for a few minutes, as usual I asked him if he was a Democrat, Republican, or Independent. He cautiously looks around to both sides to see if anyone was listening, then says, "I f***ing loooove Trump, man! He's f***ing awesome, maaan! But don't tell anyone, they might key my car or something man!" I laughed and lit up (*figuratively*), had another great conversation about our values and the crazy things going on in the world, and earned myself another voter.

Then there was a nice, beautiful woman who answered the door who turned out to be an Iranian legal immigrant. She was so thrilled when I told her I was a Republican and supported Trump. She told me all about her arduous journey her family went through coming to the United States and the pride they felt when they finally became legal American citizens. She talked about her disdain for the Democratic party's lawlessness, their encouragement of illegal immigration, and her support of Trump's America First policies, as well as building the wall. "I feel like President Trump is the first president that truly understands the effort that immigrants put in to go through the legal immigration process and he values us. It makes us respect America so much more when we put in the work and do things the right way." That house ended up being a jackpot, as she had a family of five registered voters that signed! Woohoo!

Another guy was in an apartment building. His apartment had a little buzzer with an intercom, so I buzzed a few times and finally an older man's voice picked up on the other end. He sounded annoyed and suspicious about me coming up and talking to him, but eventually and begrudgingly, he agreed to talk to me. After I told him I was a Republican, he quietly invited me in. I hesitantly stepped inside. He turned out to be such a cool man, a veteran, actually put on a MAGA hat, and showed me a whole "shrine" he had of Donald Trump memorabilia, clipped articles, and Trump gear. He called his buddy in front of me and said "Steve! Steve, you gotta hear this, there's this awesome woman at my apartment who's a Republican and she loves Trump and is running against Nancy Pelosi! You have to meet her and vote for her too!"

He, like many other Republicans I encountered in San Francisco, were so blown away by someone who was a proud patriot in such a Liberal city, because it was so rare and they were so starved for public figures who ditched the political correctness that they wanted to tell all their friends. Someone who I originally thought was going to be a grouchy old man and slam the door in my face ended up being one of my biggest fans and earned me several voters.

Through these experiences I learned that you can't have any preconceived notions about how you think someone is going to be and whether they'll be receptive to you or not. You just have to get in there and talk to as many people as possible, because it's through those great conversations that you'll earn many voters and loyal fans. Then they spread the good word about you through their own networks and families. Your influence continues to grow like a spark that grows into a wildfire.

Swearing-in My Oath of Office

Finally, 48 hours before the deadline, I completed my signatures. I was just about ready to hang my hat up for the day, but my dear volunteers really pushed me to go just a little bit longer. We really wanted to be the very *first* candidate in my race to turn in all my signatures and take my oath of office. I had a long day of door-knocking, it was raining and biting cold outside, but thanks to their encouragement, I went to one last door and it turned out to be a jackpot, as the homeowner who answered the door signed for himself, his wife, and their son, which made three signatures. That was it! I was done.

Two of my awesome volunteers who were tracking my progress immediately were alerted of the great news. They picked me up in their car right away and we went straight to the Department of Elections to turn them in, with just enough time before the office closed for the day. I handed over my many signature papers, many of which were bent and rain-stained, along with my blood, sweat, and tears in them. I filled out all the paperwork, paid the (ridiculously expensive) filing fees, and waited anxiously as the elections department staff hand counted and verified each one of my signatures.

Finally, after a long 30 minutes they came back. "Great news! You made the quota and you've qualified for being on the ballot. You've got 83 verified signatures in total, which is more than enough." I was thrilled. Then I put on my periscope and had a volunteer film me while I held up my right hand and got to take my oath of office and for the House of Representatives of the United States of America. It was such a proud moment and rite of passage that I'll always remember. AND... I was the very first candidate to take the oath of office!

I was glad that my volunteers pushed me to turn in everything then, even though I was exhausted, and not to wait until the next day, because moments after I took my oath, one of the Democratic candidates for the 12th District, Shahid Buttar, came in. He had a huge group of volunteers with him and a film crew gathering around. I hung out for a few minutes watching it and then I placed my red Trump hat back on my head that I had taken off while taking my oath. Let's just say that they did not like that! The simple act of me putting on a Trump hat caused his volunteers' collective heads to explode, some of them calling me racist and shrieking and screaming at me. One of his campaign managers finally asked me to either leave or take my hat off, because they didn't want it making a cameo appearance in his campaign videos. Finally out of respect for Shahid, I shook his hand, congratulated him, then left the room, because he deserved to have his moment in peace just like I did. It was hilarious, nonetheless.

Exhausted and cold, but glowing with pride, two of my very dedicated volunteers, and I ended the glorious day by going out for celebratory dinner and drinks in a little Irish pub with a fireplace while it stormed outside.

Door-Knocking for Getting Out the Vote

After you get your signatures, you will still be doing a lot of door-knocking, but for the purpose of meeting voters, giving them your campaign material, and asking for their vote. Hitting up hundreds or thousands of doors can get exhausting, but that's why you don't want to just go alone. You should have a team of your volunteers helping. You can have volunteers go solo or break people up into teams of two to go canvassing different precincts of your district. You can cover hundreds of doors each day with multiple volunteers canvassing for you. If the person doesn't answer, they just leave the campaign material at the doorstep and move on to the next. Ideally, you shouldn't be spending more than five minutes at each door.

Plaster the area with your campaign flyers and signage:

- Post flyers everywhere, at every lamppost you can find, bus stops, metro stations, and other public places.

- Post window signs in as many stores as you can.

- Ask local churches and community centers if you can put campaign brochures on their tables, as well as hand out brochures to people walking into and out of services and events.

- Distribute campaign yard signs to as many people as possible to put in their yards (if your district election rules allow). Unfortunately in my district of San Francisco, yard signs are not allowed, and there are tough stipulations on billboards, so I had to be more creative with building my name recognition locally.

- Distribute flyers at public transportation stations and set up a table at some of the high-traffic stations with your campaign signs, buttons, and pamphlets to distribute to as many people as possible. Have a presence at farmers markets, fairs, art shows, and any other local event in your area.

- Be present at as many local events as possible, meeting people, handing out campaign material, and asking for votes. Contact as many local clubs and organizations as possible and ask if you can speak at their next event.

Examples of places to contact, include:

- *Veterans organizations*
- *Rotary clubs*
- *Knights of Columbus chapters*
- *Women's Republican chapters*
- *Meetup groups*
- *Business networking groups*
- *Chambers of commerce*
- *Log Cabin Republicans (LCR)*

You want to get your name and face out there as much as possible! A huge percentage of why people often vote for someone is solely because they recognize their name and face. This is why if someone has been on the ballot before, they will predictably get a much larger percentage of the vote based on name recognition alone.

Identify other key communities to get votes, such as ethnic communities, nursing homes, veterans groups, and churches. In areas with large minority populations, consider creating ads in other languages. In my district, Asians made up 46 percent of the district, which is huge. So, I printed and posted up campaign ads in Mandarin, so I could help them feel included. I highly recommend having campaign material printed in other languages if there is a prominent demographic in your district, as well. Every new voter is one that you didn't have before. Other smaller communities often are tight-knit and known to spread the word within their families and networks amazingly well. If they like a person, they tend to be very loyal to that person and become an evangelist for them. I had some really awesome Asian volunteers who helped me tremendously by getting the word out about me within their communities and families, giving me advice on voter outreach strategies and translating materials. You also could consider producing a radio or TV ad in other languages on one of the high traffic stations for that demographic, budget permitting, of course.

Virtual Presence

I highly recommend making sure your virtual/technology infrastructure is set up early, so you don't have to worry about figuring out those details later in the game when you'll be much busier with physical campaigning. Technology is VERY important and necessary to reach voters.

Emailing

Your emailing platform will be the first digital piece of your voter outreach campaign that you should have in place, right from the beginning. There should be two main lists. The first contact list should include all contacts, from everywhere across the nation who you'll want to reach for fundraising efforts and campaign updates. The other list will comprise only those contacts living in your specific district who can vote for you and be mobilized to campaign and volunteer for you.

Create a call-to-action with a sign-up form front and center on your website. Signing up for your email list and donating to you, should be the only two calls-to-action on your website, social media platforms, and campaign promotional literature. Every person you meet, ask them if you can add them to your campaign email list so you can keep them updated on important campaign updates. Keep growing that list, baby. The more massive your email list, the more valuable it will be.

Consider sending email alerts for:

- Campaign updates, events, and accomplishments.
- Fundraising goals and deadlines.
- When a news interview or article is published or airs.

Texting Platform

Another essential form of communication is a strong texting platform, so you can get your messages out immediately via text. This is an essential platform to utilize, especially with the younger voters. Shop around and find a company with the lowest rates, because some companies may try to massively overcharge you. A great way to implement texting is by purchasing a specific number for your campaign. Just like President Trump with "TEXT 188-86 to be a part of Trump's Digital Army and get the latest Trump updates." Include this on your website along with your email subscriber form or in the confirmation email people receive after signing up.

Get your base mobilized early in the campaign, and let them know to follow you on your social media platforms, and to expect more texting communication from you as the campaign moves forward. Again, the time to set up your texting infrastructure is earlier in your campaign, not in the last month.

Six weeks out from your actual election is the most important period of voter communication, so you'll want to text more frequently then. Remind them that early voting begins in two weeks and include the date when it begins. Let them know *how and where* to vote and of course, to vote for YOU. Give them the URL for your website and tell them to read more about your platform and policies, as well as why you're the right candidate for them. You'll want to send at least six texts out in those six weeks leading up to your actual election. People are busy, and especially if you are a newcomer without a solid reputation in the community already, they need to be reminded to vote, and to vote for YOU!

Robocalls and Voicemail Drops

Calls and voicemails are also an essential aspect of your GOTV campaign. I chose to use both robocalls and ringless voicemail drops to get my message out to voters. Robocalls are calls directly to landlines. When the call is answered or if it goes to the answering machine, the owner hears a recorded message from you. However, since so many voters no longer have landlines, only cell phones, the "ringless voicemail drops" are pre-recorded voicemails that show up as "new voicemail" on a cell phone. The owner of the cell phone suddenly sees a new voicemail pop up on their phone, and it's a message from you.

I implemented five rounds of robocalls and voicemail drops in the month leading up to my election. I preferred recording in my own voice, so people felt like they knew me better. If you have a good "voice for radio," you should record your own. When possible, include recorded endorsements from other public figures, especially if they are local.

I chose to have calls and ringless voicemails sent out to not just registered Republican voters, but also registered "no party preference" voters, fair game in my opinion. This was a good strategy to reach voters on the fence or who may have been totally disgusted by Nancy Pelosi and the increasingly outrageous antics by Democrats, and would consider voting for a Republican this time.

This also bought in the hilarious backlash of people I called who were NOT at all happy with my message, and hated Trump. I had an assortment of people call back who left angry voicemails, prank calls, and text messages, just to scream obscenities at me. A few crazy Liberals even left death threats and yelling, "I can't believe such a *fascist* is running for office and you should be sent to a death camp along with President Putin," and "Go back to making your racist rapist America great again!"

Luckily, I don't get offended easily and I found them actually quite hilarious, even posting the most ridiculous voicemails on my social media accounts. Guess that's what happens when you campaign in one of the most Liberal cities in the country.

Election Night

Finally, the big day arrived. The days leading up to the election were crazy, stressful, and sleepless. I was getting sick as a dog, too, but fought through it and kept plugging away.

My campaign team of volunteers were nothing short of INCREDIBLE. They were out late at night stapling up posters of me everywhere, handing out hundreds of flyers at BART transit stations, churches, grocery stores, and polling stations. I wish I had gotten such a great ground team built up earlier on in the campaign, because they were true rock stars and instrumental.

I also had the mobile billboard truck driving all around the city again, flashing vibrant videos and images of me and encouraging them to vote for me.

The night before the election, we decided to hold a "virtual town hall" via phone just to make one more wave of impact with potential voters. I wanted to have people hear me talk to them live, answer any questions they may have, clear up any concerns, and see if I can sway some final votes from people who may be on the fence. I had never done one before and the technology and process was tough to learn, but a couple of my volunteers pulled together and we all figured it out. As I always say, teamwork makes the dream work!

It ended up being a really cool experience. The virtual phone banking system called out to 50,000 registered Republican voters and no party preference voters within a three-minute time frame, invited them to join my virtual town hall and ask me questions live. It was a bit nerve-wracking, because any person could ask me any question and I had to answer right there on the spot! A few people were obviously Democrats and asked me "gotcha" questions that they were hoping would cause me to crumble, but I kept my composure and answered them honestly and rationally.

The majority of people who asked me questions were respectful and actually very happy that I held the virtual town hall, saying putting a live voice to my name and that hearing me answer all the questions made them like me and trust me more, and actually earned their vote.

Finally, the big election day arrived. I was a nervous wreck and could barely sleep the night before, but I was running on pure adrenaline. I spent all day talking to people and asking for their vote.

I arrived at my election night viewing party at 8 pm, which we were hosting at Patriot House Pub. A group of my volunteers and campaign team were there and we excitedly, but nervously watched the big screen TVs awaiting the first set of results. Everyone had worked so hard and had been so supportive, but the moment of truth was now here. Finally, after much waiting, they appeared on the screen. I almost didn't want to look, because I was so scared, but my volunteers started cheering. Well, I wasn't in dead-last place at least! Nancy Pelosi was in first place, then Shahid Buttar and JD, and then there I was. The other two Democrats were behind me. It was pretty cool to see my name up there on the televisions, right next to Nancy Pelosi's I have to admit. The fact that I stayed focused and completed my race through the primary, especially after all the crap and challenges I went through, and still made it in fourth place, is a huge accomplishment.

In California, there were many dirty election laws that have been passed recently that have made it even that much harder for a Republican to win an election against an incumbent Democrat. Remember that the ridiculous "jungle primary" was a huge challenge in itself, especially being my first time running, and especially as a Republican. The other major change that California made in 2020 was to move the primary election up from June to March. That cut off three entire months to campaign, which is a huge amount of time when you're running a political campaign. Really, at the time of the primary election, I was just gaining so much ground and momentum, and having major breakthroughs in my fundraising. If I had those three extra months that candidates typically had every year prior, I know I could have pulled in thousands more votes, and perhaps even have won. Three more months would have made a huge difference!

Ultimately, I did not end up getting enough votes to pull through and move past the primary election. Guess who won instead? Aside from Nancy Pelosi of course, the radical Socialist, Shahid Buttar won second place — by quite a landslide. So now, the only two choices who will be going into the general election in November are Nancy Pelosi and the radical Socialist. There is no Republican choice now on the ticket, no Conservative voice to counter Nancy and the left. So, pick your poison!

Mr. RINO did not make it through either, even though he got more votes than me. It honestly would have been a miracle if I had gotten more votes than JD or Shahid for a number of reasons, so I wasn't totally shocked, but it was of course, very disappointing. JD already ran for that seat four times, ran for local district supervisor in his district, plus had the upper hand of being the chairman of the local GOP. He already had established years — more than a decade to be exact — of local name recognition and personally knew far more people than me locally. He had the advantage of getting to send out multiple direct mailers from the SF GOP, paid for by the SF GOP, stamped with his big name and face on it as the "SF GOP officially endorsed Republican Candidate" that went out to all the registered Republican voters in the district. That's a difficult advantage to compete with no matter how great of a candidate you are. He had the advantage of getting a major head start with his fundraising and having already years of experience fundraising, getting out the vote, and campaigning, so he had much more money to spend on advertising and more deeply embedded connections who he could have promised (or strong-armed) to vote for him. I was the new kid on the block, the outsider, and the young blood in a new city. So, considering all that I had working against me and all the advantages JD had, as well as the mafia-style intimidation and pressure tactics JD and his gang deployed to get people to vote for him instead of me, it's actually a huge accomplishment that I ended as well as I did and a bit embarrassing for him that he could not place in the top two positions.

Also, in California it is no secret that there is rampant voter fraud, election tampering, and ballot harvesting. They don't even ask for your ID when you go to vote, and California is notorious for bussing in illegal immigrants to vote and mysterious dead people rising from their tombs, who all, of course, happen to vote Democrat somehow.

It's pretty crazy that San Francisco voters, when faced with all the crap on the streets (literally), the rampant homelessness, the growing crime and drugs, on top of Nancy's horrendous actions over the course of the past year, would decide: "Yes! Give me more of THAT! In fact, give me full-blown Socialism! Bring it on!"

It's mind boggling and I can't understand it, but it appears that most of the voters in San Francisco — and much of California — are too deeply indoctrinated by the left and the mainstream media (MSM) — they truly believe that Socialism is "cool," that "Orange Man Bad," and Nancy Pelosi is their God. I did my very best to make a difference in the district and win over hearts and minds to walk away from the destructive left and see the "light" that is the "right" side, but my Congressional run was not only a political campaign, it was a sociocultural experiment. And unfortunately, the outcome of Nancy Pelosi and the radical Socialist winning the primary illustrates the social and cultural state of mind of the majority of San Francisco — and sadly, much of California.

**Make sure that you're a part of my growing community of fearless patriots as we fight together in the war of our lives to take back America. Join my Inner Circle email list and Telegram group —this is our "safe space" to freely communicate about all of these issues,*

organize, mobile rallies and other important actions that we need to take to fight back & take back America:
DeannaLorraine.com/inner-circle.

Also be sure you subscribe to my Podcast, **Taking Back America!** *I broadcast every Tuesday, Wednesday & Thursday from* **YouTube,** **Periscope, iTunes,** *and other channels and I keep you updated on the latest breaking news as well as my upcoming events.*

YouTube.com/c/DeAnnaLorraine

Twitter.com/DeAnna4Congress

CHAPTER 20

STAY ON THE FRONTLINES OF THE FIGHT

"Do what is right, not what is easy nor what is popular."
— **Roy T. Bennett**

Immediately following the primary election, the news of the novel coronavirus began dominating the airwaves. The following weeks Americans watched what looked like another seasonal flu quickly become a global pandemic. Our liberties were crept on, stores and businesses closed, and we were ordered to quarantine in our homes. This was a very confusing and frightening time for us all as we frantically watched the news and tried to make sense of everything that was happening so fast. Many public figures retreated inward and became quiet during this period. Others took a break from social media, because the news was so saturated with coronavirus-related stories and they didn't feel the topic applied to them. Not me, though. I took a different approach.

I Decided Not to Skip a Beat from My Campaign and Remain a Warrior on the Frontlines of the Fight.

I wanted to be a voice of truth, sanity, and hope for the world that people can turn to in a time where they feel lost and anxious. Plus, everyone already had gotten used to me being a thorn in my nemesis Nancy's side, calling her out when she did or said outrageous and un-American things. Now that there is no Republican choice on the ballot in my race against her, I believe it is still important, if not more so, to be a bold and outspoken Republican *voice* to counter her and the left, and guide people through winning this cultural, political, and spiritual war we're fighting.

As I always have done, I stuck to my guns, followed my instincts, and expressed my honest thoughts on these matters — and that continued to prove to be a winning strategy for me. Remember, every crisis can be turned into an opportunity to serve your community and maintain your position of leadership.

I always will be front and center, actively participating in the news and discussions around the current political and culture war every day. I wake up early and review all the latest breaking news, trending topics, and watch all of the press conferences by the president and our governors. I weigh in on the information and get everybody talking through my social media accounts, videos, and new podcast — which I stream at least three days a week. It is because I'm so active and speak my mind, that news outlets continue to call on me often for interviews, just as they did when I was running my campaign.

Remember my rule, *"well-behaved women never make history?"* And my other rule, *"trust and follow your instincts?"* Well, the validity of these rules continue to strengthen and yield success for me time and time again.

My intuition continues to enable me to see the next wave coming, catch it early, and ride it all the way through. For instance, as soon as the "impeachment season" wrapped up and the coronavirus hit, I knew it was going to be a major event, but I also knew in my gut things did not feel right about much of what we were being told. I was actually shocked and disappointed to see many political figures either parroted the same talking points and information from the MSM, or held back from expressing any dissent in order to stay politically correct and avoid getting in trouble. The message was loud and clear from most of our government, media and public figures: don't you dare question or criticize the official narrative of the coronavirus, or else you're a terrible person, you're a "conspiracy theorist," and you will be socially ostracised and banished for eternity. Oh and you're killing grandmas, too.

But my instinct was telling me otherwise. And I would rather misbehave and face persecution for the greater purpose of waking people up then keep my mouth shut and behave, knowing my silence is aiding and abetting lies. So, I wasn't very shy about sharing my thoughts and findings. I was among the first public figures to speak out about the inconsistencies I noticed that the mainstream media was reporting about the coronavirus, and what *actually* seemed to be happening with the virus. Lo and behold — even though in the beginning I was virtually tarred and feathered by hoards of people, even Conservatives — in time I proved to be on the right side of the crisis the entire time.

One of the things I noticed early on was that the mainstream media saturated our news feeds every day with horrific photos of dead bodies and freezers, death toll news tickers, and doom-and-gloom projections conveying the seriousness of the virus — reporting that hospitals were like "war zones" and hadn't been this crazy and overwhelmed since 911.

My gut told me the information was being intentionally, wildly exaggerated, so [they] could control us via their greatest weapons — massive fear and deception.

I wanted to see this "pandemonium" with my own eyes! So, one Sunday afternoon I mosied on over to two hospitals nearby with my phone to catch a glimpse, but what I saw seemed like one huge nothing burger: the hospitals looked empty, the parking lots were near empty, and the waiting rooms were near empty. Every once in a while I saw a healthcare worker coming out leisurely, looking calm and content. These did not look like healthcare workers and hospitals under extreme stress, death, and pandemonium like the news implied.

I took footage from these hospitals and posted it on my Twitter and Facebook accounts, suggesting others do their own journalism, too, and use the hashtag #FilmYourHospital.

DeAnna Lorraine ☰ ✓ @DeAnna4Congress · Mar 29

Just went to 2 hospitals in LA to check out these "War Zones" the MSM keeps telling us about. 🏥

They are very quiet & EMPTY.
We are not being told the truth. Why?? Let's get #FilmYourHospital trending. We ARE the news now. We can't trust the news. Post pics of ur hospital here!

1:01 1.4M views

○ 5.4K   ⟲ 24.2K   ♡ 32.9K   ↑   ᶁᶁ

My tweet that started the #FilmYourHospital story.

Within a few hours, the hashtag #FilmYourHospital was trending on Twitter and people from all over the country — and even all over the world — were posting videos of their hospitals, too, all of which were similarly empty and calm. Videos came in from Portugal, Italy, the UK, Chicago, and beyond. Doctors and healthcare workers even wrote in, validated my claims, and said that they were being furloughed or having their hours massively cut due to hardly any patients and not enough work!

The story was covered by many news outlets everywhere. It even inspired "Project Veritas" to go out and do their own

#FilmYourHospital video series with James O'Keefe, who produced a high-quality undercover special that went viral and was broadcasted on Hannity, Laura Ingraham, and other popular news programs. Of course, it also got me on the radar of the Soros-owned leftist media outlets, like *Right Wing Watch* and *Media Matters* and had their "commander" give their army of AstroTurf trolls the green light to come after me. I got flooded with tons of hate mail, many from supposed healthcare workers who cried that my message was "horribly insensitive" and "dangerous."

But... guess what? It sparked the conversation. A very important and necessary conversation. It got people questioning. It got people to think critically and not just blindly accept every piece of information that the MSM and "health experts" in white lab coats were spoon-feeding us. And my speaking out allowed other people to feel like they had the freedom and permission to also question things and speak out about what they were seeing.

It later came out that some media outlets, like CBS, used footage from a busy hospital in Italy, but identified the footage as being captured from New York and Philadelphia! The news outlets later admitted their culpability with a halfway apology and the people who were upset with me initially for expressing skepticism with the media's coverage realized that it was indeed warranted all along. It was clear to me that the media was hyping up the fear so that they could get us to do whatever they wanted.

Another concern that raised red flags for me right away was the "coronavirus team of experts," particularly Dr. Fauci. I got a phony and "fishy" vibe from Fauci right away, so I researched his background and dug into him more. At this point I am "woke" enough to know that just because the media and government call someone an "expert" or a "scientist" and they parade around in white lab coats with PhDs after their names, doesn't necessarily mean they are legitimate experts or have *We The People's* best interests at heart. More often than not actually, I've come to realize that many are part of the corrupt globalist Swamp, which we know has its tentacles in every industry, including the health and medical industries. Our entire country was put on house arrest, we shut down the economy, shut down businesses and restaurants, and millions of Americans were out of work and suffering. All of these extreme, unprecedented measures taken, all because of the guidance of this one man and his cronies?

We all put our trust, health, and livelihoods into this "expert's" guidance, so didn't we have a right to question and look deeper into who he was? I sure thought so. Looking deeper, it turned out he worked for the Obama and Clinton administrations and seemed to be quite chummy with all of the big Deep State players. The only solution he seemed to advocate for was vaccines, even though there were other more widely used and immediate remedies available, like hydroxychloroquine. Well, it turned out that he stood to profit big time from vaccines and a prolonged crashed economy. I pointed these things out in a few tweets along with the hashtag #FireFauci, and this also went viral around the world. Our president even retweeted my tweet calling to #FireFauci, which ended up causing a huge sh*t storm and was all over the news for weeks!

My controversial tweets even made their way into Trump's press conference, and reporters asked him specifically about my tweet that he retweeted. More and more, doctors and healthcare workers were coming forward with data and professional recommendations that were contrary to the information and predictions from Dr. Fauci, the MSM, and the Centers for Disease Control (CDC).

I had a lot to say about the MSM and the left's handling of this historic crisis, and I didn't hold back from saying it. And, guess what? Most, if not all, of the questions I raised, concerns I expressed, and predictions I shared — while they may have been called controversial or "conspiracy theories" at first — were indeed right on the money all along and ultimately proven true.

We later found out that the ominous "Covid-19 death toll" — the number of people who have supposedly died from the coronavirus that flashed in our faces every day — had been inaccurate and drastically inflated to the point of obvious fraud. We learned that, just as I suspected, most of the people who died from the virus were over age 75 and/or had coexisting conditions, like obesity or diabetes. We learned that the tests are inaccurate and unpredictable, and appear rigged to yield false positive results. It also finally came out that quarantining and wearing a mask when healthy was pointless at best, and harmful at worst and actually could cause more people to get sick — big shocker there!

I personally talked to dozens of doctors, nurses, and firefighters who all witnessed these same things, and agreed with my theory that the severity of the virus (or lack thereof) *did not necessitate* the extreme and totalitarian actions being taken. However, The Swamp and their talking heads pushed the fear so that we would willingly obey whatever ludicrous orders they were giving us.

Then, just when California and other states finally started to lift the lockdown restrictions — and people were celebrating Memorial Day in groups — Bam! The very same day, the tragic George Floyd incident happened. The world was hit with the news that an unarmed black man was killed by police officers in Minneapolis. It was horrific that he suffered a wrongful death, one that should never have happened. But, I had no more than a moment to feel empathy for what happened, before the left started hammering us with an obvious new agenda: "police are bad, and white people are still racist."

Protests and riots suddenly sprang up in major cities, as if a director yelled *Action!* and thousands of actors instantly assumed their assigned positions and executed their scripts. Forget coronavirus, a new kind of terror has been sweeping across our land. We all watched in horror as violent rioters — made up mostly of Antifa and Black Lives Matter — ravaged city after city, breaking through stores, looting everything they could get their hands on, burning down buildings and churches, and attacking anyone in their paths. We watched in terror as rioters defaced and beheaded our beloved historical monuments like a Christopher Columbus statue, the Lincoln Memorial, and the Veteran's Memorial. All while police stand down and mayors and governors do nothing except cheer it on.

All of a sudden, the virus that the "health experts" and MSM talking heads kept promising was so deadly disappeared from the news.

As usual, the radar I have for detecting BS and seeing through The Swamp's agenda started ringing loudly in my ears right at the onset. Once again, I followed my instincts and didn't waste much time before taking my thoughts public about this new horror movie called "Race Wars and Anarchy" playing in front of us.

I asked many questions:

Why did four police officers kill an unarmed man, in broad daylight, with many people around watching while they knew they were being filmed and staring right into the camera?

Why did Nancy Pelosi, Barack Obama, and other Democratic politicians immediately call for "police reform" and already have plans ready to roll out right away?

Why have health experts, the MSM, and Democrats constantly demand that we wear masks, stay in our homes, shut down our businesses, and order us against visiting friends or family because "it's too risky to spread the coronavirus," but are encouraging people to protest and riot in large masses for George Floyd?

Why have the Democrats declared that the coronavirus is so serious that they must mandate vaccines and mail-in ballots, but the virus mysteriously skips people who are rioting and protesting only for George Floyd?

TAKING BACK AMERICA

Why does the left keep screaming that "Black Lives Matter," but they won't say a word about the many black police officers who have been killed on the job by rioters? For example, retired St Louis police captain David Dorn who was killed by looters while he was protecting a friend's pawn shop.

Is all of this civil unrest really about "seeking justice for George Floyd?" How is looting cakes from the Cheesecake Factory or designer high heels from Chanel going to do anything to bring justice to George Floyd? Is this really about "Black Lives Matter" and helping the black communities? How can it be when these same people shouting "Black Lives Matter" are burning down stores owned by black Americans or killing other black Americans while rioting?

Once you're woke and you know The Swamp's agenda and how they operate, you can see things with crystal clarity and can recognize all their dirty tricks. All of the blatant inconsistencies and hypocrisies of these events are a dead giveaway that these are not naturally occurring events, but rather well-orchestrated, misinformation campaigns perpetuated by the "powers that be." What we are witnessing is a coordinated and well-funded agenda that has a nefarious purpose, but that purpose has nothing to do with our "health and safety," nor does it have anything to do with "justice for George Floyd."

This is a coordinated takeover of America.

It's no longer happening behind the scenes, though; it's happening quickly right in front of our eyes. And this

243

destruction is progressing quickly, with mobs continuing to destroy our American culture, history, heroes, and beheading and tearing down statues. They've even started making calls to blow up Mt. Rushmore and remove any statues or depictions of Jesus! This is why I follow my instincts and speak up when I get the feeling that things are amiss. This is why I really don't care if I sound stupid or crazy by calling it out how I see it. I don't care if people think I'm being a "conspiracy theorist" for sounding the alarm and sharing the truth on these matters. We're in a real war now, and we need warriors in the fight who are bold and brave enough to speak the truth so we can wake up the masses. And I know if I stand strong enough in the truth and don't waver or buckle to the pressure, the truth always comes out in due time.

As I've said from the get-go, before I even started my campaign: regardless of what happens, whether I technically win or lose my battle with Nancy Pelosi, my reasons for fighting remain the same and I will stay the course until we win the war for America's soul. I may have to adapt to the change of the waves or reposition to a different "rank," but I will remain on the frontlines of the fight.

The main lessons here are:

1. No matter what happens — whether you win or lose your election — stay on the frontlines of the fight and remain a *visible voice* who continues to make an *impact.*

2. Instead of retreating at a time of crisis — step up, adapt, and be a *LEADER* in times of crisis.

3. A Leader LEADS — even in the face of opposition and risk of persecution. A follower always follows the herd.

4. If you keep standing strong in the truth, the truth always will come out eventually and will vindicate you.

We just never really know what's going to happen in our country or the world. You can be humming along, working toward your goal, and then just like that — a situation or event happens and the world suddenly turns, the news cycle totally changes. But, it doesn't have to throw you out of the game. It doesn't have to make you disappear while you "wait your turn" again. You must learn how to be creative, agile, and adaptable — so you can ride and remain on the frontlines of the new wave in front of you.

CHAPTER 21

A FUTURE OF FREEDOM OR TYRANNICAL TAKEOVER?

"All the money and weapons in the world cannot substitute for the will to fight for our precious country and what she represents."
— **Sebastian Gorka**

A t this point in time as this book went to print, we are facing a serious turning point in American history that is more grave than ever before. The war I kept referring to when I started my campaign for Congress against the "Head of the Snake," Nancy Pelosi, was a cultural, political, and spiritual war happening mostly behind the scenes. However, now this war has moved from behind the scenes to an overt second American revolution. Will we trade our individual liberties for the promise of greater "health and safety?" Will we allow our country to be overrun by power-hungry tyrants and turned into a full-blown *Brave New World*-type police state? Will we allow the left's globalist, dystopian dream to come to fruition?

I set out on this journey to try to "save" California — or at least make an impact, so I could do my part in taking back

America. Remember, California is the "sneak peak" movie preview for everyone to watch if they want to see exactly what will happen to the rest of the country, if Democrats have their way and regain full power of the government. During the coronavirus period, destructive California policies and tyrannical Democratic leadership have been blown wide open for all to see. Ironically, while all of us have been forced to *wear* a mask, *their* masks have been lifted and they showed everyone who they really were, and their true intentions. Are you ready for this to be your reality? Because this ain't no dress rehearsal — the movie is already live in all of the blue states, and it's coming to a theater near you very soon if we don't pull the plug on it, fast.

President Trump gave our representatives an inch of power, and they have taken miles and miles. For years now, Liberals have ironically accused Trump of being a "dictator" and Hitlarian. Finally, Trump has exposed who the *real* tyrannical dictators have been all along, hiding in plain sight.

Gavin Newsom has been aggressively trying to usher in a "new normal" for California — and everyone seems to be totally fine with it except for Conservatives, who have fought it from the start. California was one of the first states to go on a statewide lockdown and close down all restaurants, stores, and businesses, and has issued some of the most draconian lockdown orders.

Despite the scientific research and God-given COMMON SENSE (or what's left of it) that it is actually *healthier* for people to be outside in the fresh air and get sunlight, Newsom thought it was a splendid idea to close beaches, parks, and public areas.

Los Angeles Democratic Mayor Eric Garcetti was so kind that he had *sand* poured in skate parks to prevent usage, because God forbid some kids who have been cooped up inside their homes all day get outside for an hour for some fresh air and exercise! He made it mandatory for residents to wear masks when leaving their homes, or risk being ticketed — yet the enormous homeless population was subjected to almost no restrictions. The ridiculous irony would be laughable if it weren't so tragic. He and other Democratic mayors like Bill de Blasio even set up "rewards" for people to snitch on their neighbors who were standing less than six feet apart, and local restaurants and businesses who dared to allow any customers inside for a few minutes. Gavin recently even banned *singing* in churches in the entire state under the guise of "stopping the spread" and have made face coverings mandatory to wear in public.

These Democratic slave drivers ordered all of us good little "civilians" to stay locked up on house arrest all day under the guise of "our safety and health," yet ordered the release of thousands of violent criminals from prisons and jails to run loose. For the life of me I don't understand the logic of this! How are we who obey the laws any safer or healthier, because of criminals released out into the wild?

An alarming 19 percent of the California workforce has filed for unemployment, with thousands out of jobs and struggling to make ends meet. Yet Gavin *Gruesome* signed a new 25 million dollar stimulus plan for illegal immigrants to help ease *their* coronavirus pains.[11] WHAT IS REALLY GOING ON?!

Like most rational people, my head hurts from trying to make sense of it. All of these actions were stupid at best, and intentionally destructive at worst. But, those of us who are woke and understand the left's playbook know that these moves are not done out of sheer stupidity — they are intentional, in order to create chaos and disorder so that they can usher in their own globalist system of "order."

After stalling as long as possible, Newsom and the Democrats finally claim to be "working toward" a re-opening of California — but with some major, frightening caveats: what they are demanding in exchange for our ability to work and live our lives again is mandatory mass health testing, "contact tracing, monitoring, and surveillance" of everyone in the state. Ummm, aren't these terms just code language for a Big Brother, Orwellian police state?

If you are like me and get an ominous feeling in your gut when you hear the term "contact tracing," your intuition is on point and you should be worried all right. Congress recently proposed a bill, called HR-6666 "TRACE" Act[12] (yes, that's really what it's called which is creepy enough as it is) that is a total nightmare. However, even though the Act hasn't even passed through the Senate or signed yet, California, along with other Democratic states, already began training "armies" of 20,000-plus contact tracers — that identify and "investigate" anyone who tests positive for coronavirus — and we now know that the "tests" can be faulty and result in a high percentage of false positives. Then these "contact tracers" demand access to all of *their* contacts and recent whereabouts, then monitor their symptoms and follow them around indefinitely — even forcibly removing people or their family members from their homes and workplaces and placing them in some kind of "alternative housing" for however long these contact tracers deem fit. There is no limit to how many times in a row they can order someone to isolate themselves, and each time they are caught in the general proximity of a person who had tested positive for COVID at one point, they are forced to quarantine for another 14 days. Their goal is to make sure every person is tested, tracked, and traced. Is this not eerily reminiscent of something that already happened in our not-too-distant history? Hitler and his Gestapo would be so proud.

In addition, The Swamp is aggressively crusading to push mandatory vaccines on all of us. Even attorney Alan Dershowitz said unabashedly in a recent interview, "If there is a pandemic and other people are at risk of getting sick, you no longer have your Constitutional rights. The State has every right to drag you out of your home and forcibly stick a needle in your arm to vaccinate you, for the good of other people." And the most horrific thing about this? The brainwashed liberal sheeple are applauding all of these stunning new invasions of our privacy and rights, because they blindly believe the words of the *powers that be* that being surveilled 24/7 is all totally normal and "just for our protection."

Remember the wise words of one of our Founding Fathers, Benjamin Franklin: *"Those who would give up essential Liberty, to purchase a little temporary Safety, deserve neither Liberty nor Safety and will lose both."*

Will the Communist tyrants soon call for curfews to be put in place, too? Will we be hauled off to jail if we don't "cooperate" with the demands of contact tracers? Before you laugh, remember that just a few months ago we wouldn't have in our wildest dreams imagined that we would willingly lock ourselves up in our homes, forced to wear face masks, nor be prevented from surfing in the ocean. We would never have imagined that we could be arrested for simply taking our own kids to the park or mourning the loss of a loved one at a family funeral.

We would never have imagined that our reality would include *talking drones* flying over the air, sounding off alarms, and barking at us if they "caught" us out in public less than six feet apart, as they're now doing in cities all over the United States. The governor of Washington State already stated that if people didn't cooperate with this mandatory testing, contact tracing, and isolation, they would not be allowed to work or leave their homes — even to go to the grocery store or to pick up essential items. Is this really America... or Communist China?!

Ironically, right before this book went to print, guess what happened? California and all other Democrat-run states across the US enforced a mandatory curfew, "to protect us from the rioting." The rioting which was caused and perpetuated by the Democrat-funded Antifa and Black Lives Matter. Others have since ordered mandatory curfews for "stopping the spread of coronavirus." Maybe I'm a little prophetic, but really, once you know the leftist globalist playbook and what their end-game is, it isn't that hard to forecast what will result from each event. I've been correct every time with my predictions, although I honestly wish I was not.

What's perhaps even more concerning than any health threat from a virus or riots, is the fact that The Swamp's big tech tyrants are working overtime to suppress any legitimate dissent to the "official coronavirus narrative," scripted by the *powers that be* and starring the WHO, CDC, and their cast of white-suited junk "scientists" and doctors. Nor can you express any thoughts questioning or critical of the scripted "Black Lives Matter — Antifa are peaceful protesters — police must be dismantled" narrative. Very prominent Conservative leaders with huge followings are getting banned and censored left and right, like Candace Owens and James O'Keefe. I'm on the chopping block, too! The tech mafia are promptly removing Facebook posts, tweets, and YouTube videos simply for dropping facts or expressing any thoughts that dissent from what the left-wing MSM, CDC, and WHO are saying. You cannot say anything negative or even truthful about Black Lives Matter, Antifa, or George Floyd. But you can bash the president all day long, you can threaten violence on any white person, and you can talk openly and endlessly about killing police or staging riots. This is modern-day book-burning and thought-policing right in front of our eyes. Call me crazy, but more and more as time wears on it sure seems that these masks we're being forced to wear are more like muzzles than "protection."

And that's very important to note: The Swamp loves to use symbols in their messaging and agendas. Think more deeply about the symbolism of a mask and of kneeling on the ground. Think about the words they have been using repeatedly every day, like "social distancing" and "new normal." The way I look at it, the mask is their symbol of obedience, silence, and control. If they can get us all to wear masks every day just because they tell us to, even when there is no science to prove its health benefits, then they are victorious over controlling us and symbolically silencing us. The "social distancing" is really social *conditioning,* conditioning us to break off our social relationships and alienate us from family and society, because they know that together we are strong, but alone and divided we are weaker. And as I talk about all the time, they know that the family unit is the strongest weapon against tyranny. If you corrupt and disrupt the family unit, you can corrupt the individuals and they are in a more vulnerable position to readily accept a tyrannical government. The new catchphrase they promptly rolled out — "I can't breath" — takes the conditioning another step further. Getting millions of people to get on their knees, wearing masks, while chanting "I can't breathe," and groveling to the Black Lives Matter "gods" begging for forgiveness for the color of their (non-black) skin tone is the ultimate act of submission and loss of individual sovereignty. And they are aggressively pushing for us to accept all of this as our "new normal."

The Next American Revolution is Upon Us

"If the freedom of speech is taken away, then dumb and silent we may be led, like sheep to the slaughter."
— **George Washington**

The coronavirus may be a legitimate virus, and a man named George Floyd may have legitimately died wrongfully. However, there's no arguing anymore that there is a significant amount of disinformation surrounding these events, too many oddities, and undeniable agendas pushed by the same Swamp players. These events are being used by the globalists as catalysts to *fundamentally alter America* and our way of life, strip us of our individual liberties, and usher in a totalitarian, technocratic, China-style government.

The "coronavirus pandemic" was used by The Swamp to:

- Crash our economy.
- Shut down small businesses.
- Blame Trump for all the damage.
- Normalize mail-in voting, which is of course easier for them to cheat.
- Enforce mass surveillance and tracking of all of us.
- Socially alienate us from others.
- Roll out mandatory vaccines, which they know kill and maim many.
- Ultimately steal the 2020 election.

The death of Floyd was the catalyst for the organized protests and riots, which became the perfect justification for governors and mayors to order us back into our homes *again* and shut small businesses right back down *again*.

The George Floyd incident also is being used as a catalyst to:

- Tear down more small businesses.
- Villainize the police, so they have an excuse to defund and dismantle the police and replace it with The Swamp's own system of "policing," which would be politicized and tyrannical.
- Keep the economy down.
- Create anarchy, fuel racial tension, and destabilize the country to usher in their own totalitarian, technocratic government.

At this moment in time, armed radical anarchists have literally taken over a section of downtown Seattle, violently drove out the police department, and designated their own separate "nation," calling it "Capitol Hill Autonomous Zone." And no one appears to be doing anything about it! The local police and the mayor are actually cheering it on, touting the anarchist takeover as merely a "wonderful, peaceful, harmless example of Democracy." This is terrifying, and if they continue to go unchecked — with Democratic leaders enabling it — you can bet, the organized anarchists will be doing the same in cities all over the United States very soon.

Remember, The Swamp needs to destroy our democracy through coordinated chaos before their plan of their technocratic, globalist new world order can take over. The masses are being played and so many gullible souls are falling right into the traps. It's a very bad sign when we have people begging for the government to step in with checks, because they can't work; begging for curfews or martial law to ease the civil unrest, and pleading for mass surveillance and vaccines in order to "stop the spread" of a so-called deadly virus. Alas, it falls right into the sophisticated plan.

Our Country is Under Attack

When we envision our country being at "war," we usually envision us being overtly invaded by foreign troops at our borders with missiles or guns pointed at us and battle tanks roaming the streets. Or we imagine there's going to be a clear declaration and a draft with a dramatic televised send off of our military.

Make no mistake though — we *are* at war. We *are* under attack. This *is* a takeover, but it's an invasion from *within*.

This is a war against the globalist, Deep State Swamp. It is a physical war now as much as it is a spiritual war and information war. You know how President Trump keeps saying that we are fighting "The Invisible Enemy?" I'm pretty sure he's not talking about just a virus. He's talking about these shadow forces and players who began their open, all-out assault on us this year.

The battle lines have been drawn.

On one side are American patriots, dedicated to freedom, preserving the Constitution, and the American way of life. On the other side are those who wish to radically transform the nation. Those who want to steal our freedom, or the leftist "useful idiots" who willingly surrender their freedom to the globalists, because they're brainwashed into believing they would be safer and better off if they're babysat and controlled by a totalitarian nanny state.

This isn't a battle of "Republicans versus Democrats" anymore. As we know all too well now, there are corrupt and compromised Swamp members on both the Republican and the Democratic side. The Swamp runs deep. Not just in our own country, but there are many tentacles of this *shadow government* that are embedded in many other countries. This is good versus evil. This is a fight that will determine whether power truly will be restored back to the people, or the people will surrender whatever little power they have left for good. And at this point in time, President Trump is the only leader fighting for our freedom. And those on the "right," although not perfect, are mainly the only ones whose hearts are generally pointing in the right direction and are fighting alongside him for our freedom. Our only shot at winning this war and preserving the America that we know and love is through uniting, fighting, and electing true Conservative *patriots*. Voting for any Democrat will only *ensure* our complete and total demise of America as we know it.

If the coup d'état that The Swamp is executing at this moment succeeds in taking over America, it will then take over the entire planet. The rest of the world looks to America as the last bastion of hope and freedom. If America falls, the rest of the world becomes dark — and our world will never be the same.

Let's look at the assets and weapons on each side: on our side, we have an anti-Establishment, patriot president who is fighting with every last breath to rebuild our country and defeat this "invisible enemy," but a very powerful, sophisticated, well-funded machine attacks him mercilessly every day and does everything it can to turn people against him.

Republicans currently are clinging to a razor-thin majority in the U.S. Senate (only *three* seats) and we're at the edge of losing it all.

On their side, The Swamp and the left have massive funding — they have billions of dollars pouring in from leftist billionaires, multinational corporations, and public-sector unions.

They have all the big tech companies on their side — Apple, Google, Twitter, and Facebook — pushing only one uniform narrative, and aggressively suppressing Conservative voices, thoughts, and facts.

They also have all the mainstream media outlets on their side, spewing anti-Trump venom, skewed polls, and false information 24/7 — even FOX news has been infiltrated by The Swamp and only a few true Conservative voices remain on the entire network.

Democrats will need to gain only three or four Senate seats to gain control, and they actually have a good chance at claiming them.

Democrats, with Nancy leading the charge, also used the coronavirus as a pitiful excuse to push for expanded ballot access and mail-in voting, crying out that "in-person voting is now dangerous to our health."

Gavin Newsom already issued an executive order to send mail-in ballots to all registered California voters for the November elections, and Michigan, Georgia, and other states are rushing to follow his lead. But we weren't born yesterday! We already know this is a recipe for fraud, ballot tampering, and illegitimate voting. In these blue states, legalized election rigging, such as ballot harvesting, absentee ballots, early voting, and same-day voter registration already will be enforced, and now they want to make it even easier to cheat. They also are going to try to push to lower the voting age to 16, and of course continue fighting for the ability of illegal immigrants (and more dead people) to vote.

The anti-American, power-hungry globalists are determined to win and regain power *by any means necessary.* All of their insidious weapons, schemes, and assets are being deployed. The deck is stacked against patriots — and this will be a fight unlike we've ever seen. This is *the most important* election in the history of America — as it will determine the future of America as we know it.

Their most potent weapons are *fear, chaos, and deception.* They have been forcing fear down our throats and engulfing us with fear, fear, fear, round the clock. They are trying to weaken us, alienate us from our relationships and families, and deflate us so we feel powerless to fight back. Fear robs us of our common sense and ability to think clearly. Fear leads us to feeling desperate and has people begging for help, for government interference, and "order out of the chaos." Fear has us willingly accepting "solutions" and infringements of our rights and liberties that we never normally would, all in the name of "our safety and protection." But remember, The Swamp are masters of *illusion and manipulation,* and they *operate in darkness.*

Our strongest weapons are *truth, unity*, and *the will to fight.* The only asset we really have on our side are *masses of people.* There are more of us than there are of them. It doesn't look like it though, and that is by their design. They create a false narrative that we freedom-lovers have very little support and we are in the minority, but that's inaccurate.

There are only hundreds of thousands of them, and millions of us. Billions if you count the rest of the world. And their greatest fear is a mass public that is *awakened* to the truth, *united, and ignited* with the will to fight. This is why they work so hard to lie to us, divide us, and break down our spirit with fear and deception. The more afraid and outnumbered we feel, the more impotent and apathetic we feel about fighting for what we want. But because they can only operate in deception and darkness, what happens when you suddenly turn the light on them? Well as the saying goes, sunlight is the best disinfectant. It's like shining bright sunlight on vampires, or pouring Holy Water on demons. They lose all their power, shrivel up, and are rendered useless. This is why the more of us that are awake and united, shining the light on them brightly and exposing them and their attacks for who they really are, the *weaker* they will be. Luckily, it appears that the events of this year have backfired on them.

"If the representatives of the people betray their constituents, there is then no recourse left but in the exertion of that original right of self-defense which is paramount to all positive forms of government."
— **Alexander Hamilton**

The entire coronavirus crisis has been a giant, ringing wake up call. The one silver lining was, more and more Americans have been hearing it and waking up. As time wore on, we rebelled: patriots across the U.S. broke out of our quarantine, questioned the narrative, ripped off our muzzles, and protested up and down California. All across America in fact, people have started waking up and fighting back. And, guess what? Despite what Dr. Fauci and the "health experts" kept warning us about, no one that I know personally has gotten sick, - although they will predictably say there are "new surges" and blame them on those of us rebelling and trying to live our normal lives. And now that we know that there is so much fraud behind the coronavirus test results and numbers, if they do declare that there are new outbreaks, which is predictable since we know their playbook, we know not to trust the numbers.

Many of us decided we would gladly take that risk in order to fight to ensure we remain a sovereign nation.

We've screamed, *"Give me liberty, or give me a (.01% chance of) death!"*

Instead of storming the beaches of Normandy, patriots have been "storming the beaches" of California. We made a stand when hundreds of us patriots ran onto Newport Beach, defied the police officers' orders, and told them that *we* were going to reopen the beach whether they liked it or not, and we were willing to get arrested for doing so. Patriots made a stand when dozens of them banded together and shoveled out the sand in the skate parks in Venice Beach that the mayor had filled in previously to make them unusable during the lockdown. We stopped waiting around for the governor's "permission" and *we* opened up the parks ourselves. Thousands of patriots of Michigan made a stand when they stormed the state's capitol building and demanded that the governor ease her draconian lockdown restrictions. Patriots of Texas made a stand recently when they protested to let Shelley Luther out of jail, the hairdresser who got arrested, because she dared to open her hair salon early.

We have been going to Black Lives Matter protests every week and standing up to them, defending our cities and our officers in blue. Thousands of us have been going to where protests or riots are scheduled to be, and worked together to board up and protect businesses from being destroyed, looted, and burned. Recently, Antifa was scheduled to show up in Placerful, California to cause destruction, and the Hells Angels rode over there and drove them off, preventing another city in ruins! Since mayors in many cities, like LA and Minneapolis, have been giving their police forces "stand down orders," business owners have been taking their protection into their own hands, standing outside their stores or on their rooftops with guns and ammunition and warding off thugs themselves. We have launched a huge movement called "Recall Gavin Newsom," and have already gathered hundreds of thousands of signatures across the state petitioning to recall California's Governor Gavin Newsom.

Those of us who are awake also have been very active battling on the digital and social media front, gaining massive ground in the information war aspect of the fight. We've been sounding the alarm, making and spreading memes, videos and information that question and expose The Swamp's agenda. Black Americans are increasingly speaking out and making videos about the fraud of Black Lives Matter and the Democratic party that have been going viral. Former organizers of Black Lives Matter have even been speaking out denouncing the organization and the left. Citizens are posting videos of piles of bricks left around town, Antifa handbooks, agitators appearing to coordinate the riots, and other things that shatter the left's narrative.

Italy has been waking up and fighting back more vocally, too! Recently, thousands of Italians gathered in Rome's Piazza del Popolo to protest against the authoritarian coronavirus lockdowns, ceremoniously throwing off their masks and declaring the pandemic a "sham." Matteo Salvini, Italy's populist party Lega Nord, led the rally along with Giorgia Meloni of the Brothers of Italy, and MEP Antonio Tajani of Forza Italia. Salvini said that the march was "a symbolic gesture to make heard the voices of the citizens who do not give up." Salvini and other powerful members of Italian parliament also have been outwardly calling out China for their many lies surrounding the virus and their "crimes against humanity."

At this moment, the leaders of the Italian populist groups have invited me to go to Italy and create a coalition of freedom-loving patriots all across the world to mobilize and fight back against those who are trying to take us over. I have talked to other patriots, too, in many other countries, and everyone is deeply concerned for America and are praying for us, because *they know* — America is the world's last hope.

People are awakening, and the match has been lit! I've come to notice that there is a distinct, intoxicating scent and vibration of energy that permeates the air when large groups of patriots are present. It is the smell of *liberation*. Many of us are now awake to the BS and illusions that have kept us asleep for so long. We see right through the devious little magic tricks that the powers that be keep trying to perform. We are filled with both anger and energy, both fear and faith, and we're fighting with every fiber in our bodies to keep our freedom that we know is on the chopping block.

We are rapidly tearing down their matrix, and "they" are losing control. But the more we tear it down, the more desperate measures they are taking to try to regain control.

We are witnessing an uprising of the resilient American spirit. We *are* making a difference, but we need to show up in greater numbers, and fight back with greater strength. We need to turn the spark that's been lit into a roaring, unstoppable fire that sweeps over our nation and spreads to other countries. We can make an even bigger impact if many more of us wake up and have the courage to walk through the fear and fight back. Remember, there are more of us than there are of them.

We have the power to render their weapons powerless if enough of us do not submit nor react to their attacks in the ways they are hoping we will.

Their fear and propaganda will no longer be effective if there are more people who see right through the lies than people who believe them. We need at least 60 percent of the population awake in order for our voices to be loud enough and our efforts formidable enough. Their authoritarian orders and attacks no longer can work if there simply aren't enough people who buy into them. If enough of us *refuse* to cooperate with this unconstitutional "contact tracing" program, and make enough noise, we can nullify the entire operation. Their attempts to weaken and castrate "white" people and destroy American nationalism using the guise of "systemic racism" will simply not work if enough people refuse to apologize for crimes we never committed and the color of our skin.

We can make a significant stand if enough businesses, churches, and restaurants defy the lockdown orders and re-open regardless, and enough of us stand by their sides and go to bat for them. We can make a stand by being brave enough to refuse to be tested, traced, or vaccinated, even when faced with being arrested or fired. Their false flags, race wars, and other events meant to divide us or chip away at our rights can be neutralized if enough people learn to recognize right away the markings of these coordinated events, and simply *stop giving them the reaction* that they expect. And for God's sake, we can prevent the violent anarchists taking over our cities one by one if enough of us patriots mobilized together, took up arms, and stopped them in their tracks! The anarchist takeover happening in Seattle should never, ever have been allowed to happen — but make no mistake, it *will happen* to all of our cities, soon, if we don't wake up, unite, and fight back. The other side has fewer numbers than us, but are highly organized and funded. We have more numbers by far, but because we aren't well organized and many of us have become apathetic or paralyzed by fear, those numbers are meaningless. There is strength in numbers, and if there are enough of us badasses fighting the tyrants, then what are they going to do, fire and arrest us all?

It is predictable that they will keep throwing more attacks at us. It's going to get uglier and bumpier as we progress in this war. *No one said it would be easy* to take back our beloved country that's been hijacked by a powerful evil group of monsters who are out to destroy everything that we stand for and that God intended for our destiny. If we don't have the courage to stand up for what we believe in now, then when? If we don't have the will to fight to take back our country now, then when? What or who are we waiting for? There's no hero on a white horse coming to rescue us. And we cannot even wait for the president to swoop in and save us. We need to rise up and be our own heroes who will be etched into the history books as the brave ones who fought to take back America.

Remember, "The people shouldn't be afraid of their government. The government should be afraid of its people."
— **V, V for Vendetta**

We need to push through fear and become FEARLESS.

Remember when I was afraid, and I allowed myself to be held a hostage? I allowed myself to be weakened and controlled by fear, and I gave up my power to the enemy; which only emboldened them more. When I stopped letting fear take over me, I gained back my power. Remember, *The threat is usually more terrifying than the thing itself.*

As fighters for freedom in this next American Revolution, we must walk through that fear with courage, knowing that the faith and fire in our hearts comprise the most powerful weapon that kills any perceived threat.

This is truly our last shot at freedom.

This is why I fight. This is why I need to keep on fighting. This is why *we* need to rise up, unite, and fight. This is why we need to be fearless and outspoken, shining the truth brightly against the dark enemies and keeping them fully exposed so they have nowhere to hide, and shrivel up and die. This is why we must break down the corrupt "Old Guard," and install a "New Guard" of fierce, freedom-loving, Constitution-honoring patriots. No more old Establishment, deepstate puppets. No more perfect-on-paper, but wolves in sheep's clothing representatives. We need to stop caring about the "appearance of perfection." Remember folks, we are not electing people to be pastors and nuns here. The future of our Republic is at stake here, and the main credentials we need from this new future of leaders are passionate patriotism, good hearts, and a fearless, fighting spirit.

This is the story of true American patriots; the outsiders, the rebels, coming together and standing up to *fight* the Establishment, fight the globalist agenda, and take back our America that we know and love. *You* are part of this story. What part will you play? Will you play the part where you sit back and do nothing? Will you play the part where you keep voting in the same old tired politicians who will continue to send our country into the history books? Or will you play the part that joins me in this fight and supports me in turning OUR country around — and have our American story continue?

We are capable of preserving this next generation and saving this crumbling empire. The question is, will you be bold and take on this task? Will you join me in this fight?

It's up to US. This is the war of our lifetime. And together, we WILL win this fight.

I may not have "won" my election, but it is only one of many battles in this war to take back America. And I know I've made a difference. I will continue fighting and striving to make a difference, so we can ultimately win this war. I hope I've inspired you and other people to take greater action on the frontlines, run for office, or be a bolder voice of truth and patriotism. YOU can make a difference!

And that makes it all worth it. I've been through a hell of a battle. I've made some mistakes and I'm still learning and growing, but I wouldn't take it back for anything. And, if I decide to run for office again, I will be much wiser, better, stronger, and more fearless.

I'm not going anywhere. I will be here on the frontlines, fighting for God, family, and taking back our incredible country. And... the *best is yet to come.*

**Make sure that you're a part of my growing community of fearless patriots as we fight together in the war of our lives to take back America. Join my Inner Circle email list and Telegram group —this is our "safe space" to freely communicate about all of these issues, organize, mobile rallies and other important actions that we need to take to fight back & take back America: DeannaLorraine.com/inner-circle.

Also be sure you subscribe to my Podcast, **Taking Back America!** *I broadcast every Tuesday, Wednesday & Thursday from* **YouTube**, **Periscope, iTunes,** *and other channels and I keep you updated on the latest breaking news as well as my upcoming events.*

TWITTER: @Deanna4Congress

YouTube.com/c/DeAnnaLorraine

AUTHOR BIO

Ms. DeAnna Lorraine is a Conservative political firebrand and recent Republican, "anti-establishment" Congressional Candidate who just completed her widely watched run against political Goliath Nancy Pelosi in California's 12th Congressional District (San Francisco). She is also a popular YouTube Host, Political and Culture commentator, Author, and Host of her podcast and Internet show "Taking Back America with DeAnna Lorraine." She is known for talking boldly about the destructive impacts of Liberalism and Feminism and how they're destroying our relationships, the family – and our country on the whole. DeAnna makes frequent media appearances (Newsmax, CNN, FOX, OANN, The Blaze, The Daily Caller, etc), and has given riveting speeches at the Walkaway March, the American Priority Conference, the Eagle's Council, the #DemandFreeSpeech Rallies, and many other major Conservative events.

Follow DeAnna Lorraine:brea

TWITTER: @Deanna4Congress

WEBSITE: www.DeannaLorraine.com

YouTube.com/c/DeAnnaLorraine

BIBLIOGRAPHY

1. DeAnna Lorraine, *Making Love Great Again: The New Road to Reviving Romance and Winning at Relationships* (Los Angeles, CA: 4th Street Media, 2018)1

2. Donna Calvin, "The 45 Communist Goals as Read Into the Congressional Record in 1963," *BeliefNet.com*, https://www.beliefnet.com/columnists/watchwomanon thewall/2011/04/the-45-communist-goals-as-read-into-the-congressional-record-1963.html (accessed April 2, 2020)

3. MinutemanDavid, "The 11 Step Plan of Cultural Subversion," *State Militia Intel*, September 10, 2019, https://statemilitiaintel.wordpress.com/2019/09/10/t he-11-step-plan-of-cultural-subversion/

4. United Nations, "Transforming our world: the 2030 Agenda for Sustainable Development," *Sustainable Development Goals*, https://sustainabledevelopment.un.org/post2015/trans formingourworld (accessed April 11, 2020)

5. CBS News, "California clears way to provide health care to some immigrants," *CBSNews.com*, June 10, 2019, https://www.cbsnews.com/news/california-clears-way-to-provide-health-care-to-some-immigrants/

6. Alicia Victoria Lozano, "How California's homelessness crisis surged," *NBCNews.com*, January 25, 2020, https://www.nbcnews.com/news/us-news/no-one-catch-us-how-california-s-homelessness-crisis-exploded-n1123156

7. Dominic Fracassa, "SF blacklists 22 states for anti-choice abortion policies," *San Francisco Chronicle*, October 16, 2019, https://www.sfchronicle.com/bayarea/article/SF-

blacklists-22-states-for-anti-choice-abortion-14537449.php

8. Allan Smith, "Parents guilty of murder and raised by radicals, Chesa Boudin is San Francisco's next district attorney," *NBCNews.com*, December 16, 2019, https://www.nbcnews.com/politics/elections/parents-guilty-murder-raised-radicals-chesa-boudin-san-francisco-s-n1101071

9. Stephen Frank, "Marso: Plan to Revitalize San Fran GOP," *California Political Review*, June 25, 2020, http://www.capoliticalreview.com/capoliticalnewsandviews/marso-plan-to-revitalize-san-fran-gop/

10. Jesse McKinley, "The Republican Actually Running Against Pelosi," *The New York Times*, October 9, 2010, https://www.nytimes.com/2010/10/10/us/politics/10dennis.html

11. CNBC, "California announces $125 million fund for undocumented immigrants impacted by coronavirus," *CNBC.com*, April 15, 2020, https://www.cnbc.com/2020/04/15/california-to-give-cash-payments-to-immigrants-hurt-by-coronavirus.html

12. United States Congress House Bill, "H.R.6666 - COVID-19 Testing, Reaching, And Contacting Everyone (TRACE) Act," *Congress.gov*, May 1, 2020, https://www.congress.gov/bill/116th-congress/house-bill/6666/text